RONNIE SELLE

81 West Commercial St., Portlanc

MW01611059

May 2005

A note to the reader:

If you are among the 50 million North Americans who will turn 50 during the next 10 years, *Fifty Things To Do When You Turn Fifty* might just be the thing that enables you to approach the experience with optimism rather than dread. In fact, after reading it, I would go so far as to say no one should attempt to turn 50 until after they've read this book! I should know. I turned 50 several years ago, before the book was available, and the experience almost caused me to come unglued.

The artists, pundits, and experts who contributed essays have offered a wealth of practical information, to be sure. When taken collectively, the book comprises a veritable instruction manual for how to turn 50, everything from how to readjust your stock portfolio to how to readjust your underwear (to allow for more breathing room . . . wearing comfortable clothing is, after all, a privilege that you have more than earned by now).

But the practical information, as useful as it is, is not the most valuable aspect of this book. Rather, it is the hopeful, upbeat feeling you are left with after reading what each of the authors has to say about his or her big 5-0 experience. The underlying message is: relax, now that you're 50 you don't have to prove yourself anymore. Take care of yourself, get your house in order, and these will be the best years of your life.

I think you'll agree that this is a message anyone turning 50 will find both soothing and encouraging!

Sincerely,

Ronnie Sellers
President and Publisher

FIFTY EXPERTS ON THE
SUBJECT OF TURNING FIFTY

FIFTY
Things To Do
When You Turn
FIFTY

Contributing Editors Alison Kyle Leopold •
Gerit Quealy • Debra Gordon • Brian
O'Connell • *Series Editor* Sarah Mahoney

Ronnie Sellers Productions, Inc.

P.O. Box 818, Portland, Maine 04104

For ordering information:

(800) 625-3386 toll-free

(207) 772-6814 fax

Visit our Web site: www.rsvp.com • E-mail: rsp@rsvp.com

Ronnie Sellers: President and Publisher

Robin Haywood: Publishing Director

Mary Baldwin: Production Editor

Jessica Curran: Associate Editor

Design by: The Design Works, Sisters, Oregon

ISBN: 1-56906-590-X

Library of Congress Control Number: 2005TK

10 9 8 7 6 5 4 3 2 1

Printed and bound in Leominster, Massachusettes
by Quebecor, Worldwide

Contents

SECTION THREE
REDEFINING FITNESS

SECTION FOUR
STAYING STRONG

SECTION FIVE
MANAGING YOUR CAREER AT MIDLIFE

SECTION SIX
MASTERING YOUR MONEY

SECTION SEVEN
HAVING FUN LIKE A GROWN-UP

Section Eight
Watching the Big Picture

Section One

FINDING YOUR
50-SOMETHING
ATTITUDE

1

Stop complaining

**No one cares that you don't like getting older —
so quit bellyaching. But 50 is a great time to lose
the ponytail, start telling the truth, and stop having
dinner with people you don't like.**

BY GARRISON KEILLOR

Keillor is the host of A Prairie Home Companion which is
heard Saturday nights on public radio stations around the
country, and lives in St. Paul, Minnesota.

When you hit 50, you have to stop complaining about getting old, the strangeness of it, the fascination, the horror, etc. etc. That was okay in your 30s and 40s, but now that you're old, it's time to shut up on the subject. The term "senior moment," for example, or joking references to your prostate, or Alzheimer's: stifle it. You shouldn't complain about aging for the simple reason that nobody gives a hoot. If you were to pay people to care, they might care a little bit for an hour or two, but you didn't and they don't. So learn to be cheerful about it. When someone asks how you are, tell them, "Absolutely great. Never better."

Fifty is the time to try giving up television and newspapers and radio for six months or a year and see what the simple unmediated life of direct experience is like. You won't know if you don't try.

By 50, everyone can stand to lose 20 pounds, so do it. The simplest way is to adopt a new philosophy of eating, which is revolutionary in America but which is essential for an older person: eat to satisfy hunger; if you're not hungry, don't eat. Stop eating when your hunger is satisfied. Except on Sunday or whichever day is your feast day. As you get older, your metabolism changes and now you can sustain yourself quite well on one meal per day and two snacks. So that's what you do.

Fifty is the time to take a long hard look in the mirror. Especially for the aging bohemian. A young person is allowed to dress up as Desperado, Punk Princess, Noir Poet, or Frontiersman, but by the age of 50 you've wised up. You've seen how ratty those old ponytails get to looking. What was revolutionary at 21 can be rather stringy and pitiful at 50. What works for Willie Nelson doesn't necessarily work for you. So you look at yourself and maybe you adopt a new look and do it in a totally cool way, no comment, no angst, just shave and shower and cut the hair short and drop some weight, start running, put on a jacket and tie, and if jaws drop, you just say, "Hey, why not?" You do not compromise your principles one degree, you don't tone down your views, you simply adopt a more conventional look, which might free you up in all sorts of ways.

Put the past behind you. This is even easier to do at my age (62) but you can get a start at 50 — make a pile of your regrets and put a match to them and let them blow away, the lost loves, the estranged friends, the botched education, the unwritten novel, the neglected guitar, the ruinous investments, the dear friend who committed suicide, the opportunities that sailed away without you — put that knapsack full of rocks on the ground and walk away and find something in the here-and-now that absorbs you and take up with that, a garden, a grandchild, a choir, yoga, knitting, amassing a collection of porcelain pigs, political agitation, learning the drop-thumb style of banjo.

Start telling the truth. In small doses at first and then gradually build up to one out of three, a decent batting average. When you're young, you're scared, you're trying to wend your way through the trees and not get shot at, you're trying to stay on the warm side of the various big cheeses in your life, you're wanting to be the good guy who everybody loves, not the jerk with the big mouth. But when you hit 50, you're entering a new passage of life in which you can say what you really think. You can express outrage at the shameful things that take place in this dear land, the shabby treatment of the poor and the young, the gorgeous favors bestowed on the rich, the swift growth of government under our conservative regime.

You can also dare to express simple preference. Do you want to go over to the Swansons for dinner? No, I don't. Why not? I thought you liked them. They complain constantly about aging and I'm tired of looking at his hair. Oh. Okay. What would you rather do? Lie on a bed with you and talk and drink a little wine and listen to Frank Sinatra with the lights out. Oh. Okay.

Speaking of wine, 50 is also a good time to take an honest look at the beverages in your life. The miseries of alcohol are probably clear to you by now, and so you might, as an intellectual and spiritual exercise, take a vacation from booze and learn to appreciate the world's panoply of excellent teas. For most people, this will be a struggle, but there is something to be gained, and that is simplicity. If you worry about alcohol, then you probably have good reason to, and that is enough reason to take a vacation. Refrain for a month and that will make the next month easier and soon you'll be to six months and a year, and after that, it's not so hard: not drinking is easy so long as you don't drink.

Fifty is an excellent age for reform of all sorts. You have enough experience and good judgment to know something about yourself and you can see the end of your life from here and so, gauging your desires and your strength, you adjust and straighten and balance and alter what needs altering and press on. It's a time of marvels on every hand, great richness, emotional clarity, and great sweetness. Sixty is even better, but don't hurry.

2

Look for what's hopeful and go with it

At 50, you've got plenty of reasons for optimism.

BY WENDY WASSERSTEIN

Wasserstein is one of the most influential woman writers and playwrights working today. A native New Yorker, her plays include The Heidi Chronicles, which won the Pulitzer Prize and the Tony Award. Her new play, Third, opens at Lincoln Center in the fall of 2005.

I used to make lists at every decade birthday of what I wanted to do, what I felt I needed to accomplish. But I didn't make one when I turned 50. I think between 40 and 50, I learned a lot more about life. My oldest sister Sandra died of breast cancer when I was 47. My daughter Lucy Jane was born ten weeks early when I was 49. So I sort of started seeing the ridiculousness of lists.

Not that lists are necessarily ridiculous in and of themselves. I know that you can plan some things. But you can't plan others. And you begin to think about luck æ what's lucky and what's not. That may be unfortunate because it means that I agree with my friend [playwright] Christopher Durang that life is random.

I didn't like turning 50 very much. I remember having a party when I turned 40, but also being very anxious, because my life had been so much more focused on my career, rather than on my personal life. I thought, there's all this stuff I've still got to do. I've got to get a home, I have to have a child. Turning 50 was harder because my sister had died, and my Dad was sick. It just was harder æ there was a lot of real life going on. With so much loss, it became about survival. Of course if your sister and your father and your best friend die, what are you supposed to do? It made me think, what's precious to me? What do I really care about?

By the time you're 50, certain things have less importance in your life, in terms of aging, for instance, especially if you're a woman. Unless you're a movie star, unless you're used to being Cate Blanchett all your life (which would be a different thing; I'm sure that must be hard too). If you're Wendy Wasserstein and you turn 50, it's not like you say, "I really miss that figure." I just thought, "I am who I am. It's just fine." That was quite liberating.

And then the big question æ what am I going to do when I grow up? There always seemed to be an endless amount of time to answer that. When you're 50, you know there isn't an endless amount of time. You just know it. But you still have to believe that you can change things. If you didn't believe you could change things, it would be horrible.

So you find things to get you through. You try to have a

strong-enough backbone. And you try not to get hysterical. A sense of humor is essential because it's not fake. Unless it's a laugh track on television æ when someone says, "I'm crossing the street," and you hear laughter. Obviously there's no laugh track in life. If you're really funny, it means there's a lack of pretense, a sense of humanity. It's an understanding that you're not that important. "It" is not that important. Self-importance can be a dangerous thing.

At this juncture, I suppose some women feel reborn and ready to go, with their family grown, and that they're entering into a wonderful third phase of their life. If you try to be positive, you have to think there are new things to learn. You get scared of becoming entrenched, not meeting new people, expanding in new ways. But what I've found most useful since I've turned 50 is that the things that I feel are deep in my life have gotten deeper. My friendships with the people I really like have become deeper. I'm much less interested in parties and connections. I feel much closer to my friends. I try to spend more time with my daughter. I'm closer to my work. The things I really care about. I've gone deeper into what's there.

I've said that I'm nice in a sometimes-rueful way. But now I think "nice" has gotten a bad connotation. I think nice is nice. Nice has gotten a bum rap as sort of not sexy, not edgy, not interesting. In fact, kindness can go a long way.

You have to decide there's hope. I think there's hope in acceptance, too. For instance, I wrote an article for More magazine about turning 50, saying that for a 50-year-old woman, hope comes with a lot of history, a degree of disappointment, some skepticism, and a great deal of depth.

And as I've said before, you have to just show up every day and hope for the best. You do the best that you can æ that is really how I feel about being 50. For someone turning 50, I would say and this is in a new play of mine "Go with the hope." Look for what's hopeful, and try to find that hope. ☀

3

Write your own top ten list

You don't have to be David Letterman to come up with your own list of 10 great things about turning 50.

BY PATRICIA FARRELL

Patricia A. Farrell is a licensed psychologist and a regular on such national TV shows as The View, The Maury Show, The O'Reilly Factor, and CNN. The native New Yorker is also the author of How to Be Your Own Therapist (McGraw-Hill).

Bette Davis said "Old age is no place for sissies," and at 50, I've come to believe her. I've also come to believe that 50 is the new 30, as least as far as I'm concerned. The dread I recall when I was approaching my 30th birthday was clearly out of proportion to anything that actually happened on or after that fateful day. So when 50 rolled around, it was a piece of cake in every sense of the word. I was now firmly planted in adulthood and, clearly, my own person in my own career. Who would have thought?

Of course, we psychologists have a way of looking at most things, even the aging process, as positive rather than negative. So my birthday gift to you is to pass on some of that positive thinking to get you beyond any lingering anxiety you might have about this momentous age.

I'll do that with my own personal list of the top 10 positive things about turning 50. Read them carefully and you'll understand why I believe we should all view this milestone as a beginning of something new.

10. You no longer have to worry about what your parents will say if you don't come home on time. In fact, you don't even have to go home if you don't want to. The glorious part about turning 50 is that you're now into that part of your life in which the family "elders" can no longer make you feel anxious or guilty with their dire pronouncements about what you're doing (or not doing) with your life (you may even be the family elder). Today, what you do with your life is your responsibility—no one else's. If you want to, as they say, "go to hell in a hand basket," it's your choice.

9. You can read whatever you want, whenever you want. Be it trashy novels or literary classics, both feed your brain and enrich your life. You're old enough to know that now, so pig out at the bookstore and read what you want. No more hiding "trashy" books under your bed, in the closet, or out in the garage. After all, you're 50 and your own person! Besides, you can tell them, studies show that reading helps stave off Alzheimer's disease. So let Danielle Steele, or any other writer you like, come to your cognitive rescue.

8. Your financial life and financial future are in your

hands. After all, you're the one earning the money and paying the bills. No more asking if you can go anywhere or buy anything. It's up to you to decide how good or bad you'll feel afterwards. Anyway, what's wrong with one of those delicious impulse purchases?

7. You can eat anything you want for breakfast, be it birthday cake, cold pizza, Chinese food, or even souvlaki. Breakfast, after all, is the most important meal of the day. That doesn't mean, however, that you have to observe the usual rules all the time. In fact, cereal for dinner also sounds good!

6. You no longer have to worry about keeping up with what's current in music and you can dance the way you want to. Like the music of the 70s, 80s, or even 40s? Let it rip and play it in your car, your home or your office. As Barbra Streisand once said, "This is the only music that makes me dance." So dance away wherever or whenever you want.

5. You no longer have to put on make-up (or hold your stomach in) before you put the garbage out. It's okay for your neighbors, the garbage man or anyone else to see that, indeed, you do not awaken as they do in film—fully made up.

4. You can declare Sunday to be an absolute day of rest without guilt. One of the perks of being a grownup. So spend the seventh day in bed with the newspapers, cookies, chocolate, or submarine sandwiches if you want. It's your

day and you make the rules.

3. You no longer have to consider golf a competitive sport. By now, the game should just be fun. If anyone else doesn't realize that, it's up to you to educate them. In fact, at this time in your life, second-hand clubs are more fashionable than the latest technology because they show you care not a whit for impressing anyone and that the game, not the trappings, is what's most important.

2. You no longer have to adhere to some unrealistic idea of thinness. Free yourself from unrealistic ideas about dieting until you fit into clothes you deliberately bought too small. You know what's comfortable and healthy and you have the brains and the will to take care of yourself. Today's diet expert is tomorrow's has-been.

1. You no longer have to answer that question we all hate: What are you going to be when you grow up? You're all grown up now and, if you want to change careers, that's okay, too. No one can make you keep on doing something you absolutely hate.

It's also time to realize some of those long-held wishes. What will it be. . . a Hawaiian vacation? Skiing in the Rockies? Shopping for hidden treasures in those little out-of-the-way markets that dot the side roads of America? Stop wishing and start planning.

Enough words of wisdom from a psychologist? If not,

here are a few more. The fact that you've reached 50 and are reading this book is a milestone in and of itself. It shows that you've done pretty well with your life up to this point. I urge you to continue seeking the joy in life and reframing the setbacks. Remember, whenever you're not sure if you should do something spontaneous, buy something frivolous, or say something silly, just tell yourself: "I've earned it!"

4

Go ahead, be melodramatic

The former poet laureate comes to terms with the fact that immortality is unlikely.

BY BILLY COLLINS

Collins served as the US Poet Laureate for 2001-2003, and has won the Oscar Blumenthal Prize, the Levinson Prize, and a Guggenheim Foundation fellowship. His poems appear regularly in publications such as The New Yorker, The Paris Review, and Harper's. He has published over seven volumes of poetry; Questions About Angels won the National Poetry Series publication prize.

Poetry has as many subjects as there are things in the world around us, but the underlining subject of poetry, as every English major knows, is Death. In fact, anyone who decides to major in English should be advised that they are actually majoring in Death. So for poets, every day is a good day to write a poem on mortality, but the occasion of a birthday brings the subject into sharp focus, and if the birthday number ends in a zero...well, poets are apt to feel a professional obligation to mark the event with some utterance in verse. The following is my response to turning 50, and the chilling thought of it, as the end of the poem makes clear, was enough to scare me back into the arms of the Church, or at least into the grip of her language.

Fiftieth Birthday Eve

The figure alone is enough to keep me wide awake,
the five with it's little station master's belly
and cap with the flat visor, followed by the zero,
oval of looking glass, porthole on a ghost ship,
an opening you stick your arm into and feel nothing.

I want to daydream here in the dark, listening
to the trees behind the house reciting their poems,
bare anonymous beings, murmuring to themselves
in lines that reach out like long branches in spring.
I want my mind to be a sail, susceptible to any breeze
that might be blowing across the lake of consciousness.

But I keep picturing the number, round and daunting:
I drop a fifty-dollar bill on a crowded street,
I carry a fifty-pound bag of wet sand on my shoulders.
I see fifty yearlings leaping a fence in a field,
I fan the five decades before me like a poker hand.

I try contemplating the sufferings of others, Rossini,
for example, considered by many to be the Father
of Modern Insomnia for his prolonged sleeplessness
during the composition of the William Tell Overture.

But even a long meditation on the life of Brahms,
widely recognized as the Father of the Modern Lullaby,
will not dispel the fives and zeros, gnomes in the night
perched on the bedposts, one straddling a closet
doorknob.

By dawn, I have become a Catholic again,
the oldest altar boy in the parish, complete
with surplice and cassock, cruet, thurible, and candle.

And this day, whose first light is gilding the windows,
has become another one of the sorrowful mysteries,
following the agony in the garden of childhood
and preceding the crucifixion,
the letter X removed from the word and nailed
to a cross,

the rest of the alphabet standing witness
on the rocky hillside, marveling at the lightening
that is cutting silently across the dark sky.

-from The Art of Drowning,1995, University of Pittsburgh Press

5

Keep a sense of adventure

**At midlife, most of us face a fork in the road.
It's up to us to decide whether to take the easy ride,
or the uncertain one to spiritual rebirth.**

BY MARIANNE WILLIAMSON

Williamson has published eight books including the bestseller
A Return to Love. Three other books reached No. 1 on the
New York Times bestseller list, and include Illuminata,
Everyday Grace, A Woman's Worth, and Healing the Soul of
America.

I found turning 50 harder than I expected it to be.
Somewhere around two or three months before the big
day, I started to be haunted by memories of a youth now
irrevocably over. As much as I told myself that 50 is the new
40, what I really wanted in my heart was to have the old 40
back. I had waking nightmares of blazing memories – things
I hadn't handled well, stupid choices I had made and could
not make over, chances I thought were never more to be
retrieved. Grieving the glory of my younger years, I had to
face myself and all the pain that comes with that.

Several friends told me they had experienced the same thing, but not to worry – all of a sudden the anxiety would lift. And indeed that is the way it happened for me. Sitting at an outside cafe late on the night of my big five-O, looking up at the Eiffel Tower lit up against the sky, I felt the pain lift. In an instant, it was all okay. I knew the sun had set on what was no longer, but I had a sense that something new would now dawn to take its place.

Girlfriends had told me that the 50s are great because you don't care anymore what others think. I don't know if that will be true for me, but I do know that I'm not who I used to be. Fifty is as different from 40 as 40 is from 30 and 30 from 20. With the coming of 50, one makes a transition as fundamental as that of puberty. I have settled into the paradox of middle age.

On one hand, you finally have some sense of what you're doing in the world. At last I'm convinced I have a right to be here. I'm not as frantic as I used to be, though I can't tell yet whether that's because I've evolved or just aged. On the other hand, I get tired more easily, I often can't remember things, and I'm exhausted just from looking for my glasses all the time! Most disconcerting of all, when I'm a serious mood and I do the math, I can't garner much hope of changing things on this planet during the time I have left. Our generation's shared delusion that we would usher in paradise has been completely shattered. The older you get, the more you see how entrenched certain negatives are. There is so much cruelty in the world that you thought for years would go away; and as you age, it dawns on you that it never really does.

As disillusioning as it is to realize these things – and disillusionment is actually a good thing because it means you were laboring under illusions before – it's also the beginning of spiritual insight. Once you're deeply convinced there are no ultimate answers outside yourself, you start looking for them where they truly are: inside. And you realize that in your slowing down, you're more prepared to listen to things you were moving too fast before to hear.

So much wasted time, so many stupid mistakes. You feel you have the knowledge now, but you're not sure you have the energy left: if only you had known then what you know now. You come to understand George Bernard Shaw's comment, that "Youth is wasted on the young."

Our adrenal glands decimated, our cells like fast cars beginning to show wear, the fastest generation has begun to slow down. Jack Nicholson said in a recent interview, "My generation is the new old." Our deepest burden is the accumulated sorrow, the heartbreak of one decade impinging upon the next until the heart can absorb no more. Your mind has figured so much out, but your body isn't sure that it cares anymore. When it's more depressing than joyful to wake up in the morning, then you know you have a problem.

And many people do.

Most people, once they hit middle age, face a fork in the road. And which road they take, in the words of Robert Frost, will make all the difference. One road leads to gradual dissolution — a cruise however slow toward death. The other road becomes a birth canal, a pattern of spiritual rebirth. The older we get, the harder it is to choose rebirth.

The ego's gravity seems harder to resist.

We start out so enthusiastic about life, so entertained and delighted by the very nature of things. But the newness fades; we grow jaded or exhausted, and we begin to lose some vital appreciation for the possibilities inherent in a day. As I write this, I hear teenagers in my backyard, delighting in the mud puddles produced by the afternoon's storm. I have to consciously check myself – to remind myself that the ability to have fun in the mud is what makes being young so wonderful, and not make a stink about the fact that my towels are beige and this could ruin them. My mortal truth is that I want the kids to hose off before they come back into the house, but my soul's truth is that I wish I could enjoy the mud too.

So it's completely up to me, whether I start to become an old biddy who cares too much about the towels, or instead hold on to my sense of adventure and remember what's important. What the hell, the kids are happy and that is what's important. And not just for kids, but for all of us.*

*Reprinted with permission from A Gift Of Change, Harper Colllins San Franciso, 2004**

Section Two

MAKING PEACE
WITH THE MIRROR

Stop obsessing about your flaws

The only beauty secret that matters is learning to look more like you, and less like somebody else.

BY BOBBI BROWN

The founder and CEO of Bobbi Brown Cosmetics was working as a makeup artist in New York when she launched her company — with just 10 brown-based lipsticks — in 1991. These quickly gained a strong following first among beauty insiders, then women everywhere.

As I look to turning 50, I can finally say that I've come to terms with myself, and I hope the things I've learned along the way will help other women see their own beauty.

When I was 13 years old, I wanted to look like Cheryl Tiegs. She was tall, thin, and blonde the epitome of beauty in the late 1960s. Standing at just five feet tall, with dark brown eyes, dark brown hair, and strong eyebrows, I couldn't have looked any more different. I spent a lot of time feeling bad about this until I saw Ali MacGraw in the movie Love Story. Those dark eyes, that hair and those thick eyebrows.... in her I finally saw the possibility of my own beauty. This realization changed how I viewed myself, how I saw other women, and it ultimately led me to my career as a makeup artist.

My love and obsession with makeup began at age six when my mother gave me a box of her old cosmetics, a pad of paper and the instructions to have fun drawing while she prepared dinner. Instead, I chose to make up all my dolls and stuffed animals to perfection. At 16, I landed my first job at a small makeup boutique. As part of my orientation, the owner gave me a makeover to "correct" what she saw as my flaws she applied pink foundation to cover my too-yellow skin; shaded my nose to make it look smaller; tweezed my brows into thin, sparse lines; and outlined my lips outside my natural lip line to "create fullness." I couldn't wait to go home to wash my face when I saw my reflection in the mirror.

When I look at a woman, I don't see what's wrong with her, I see what's right and that's why I'm troubled by the current definition of beauty that favors a cosmetic surgery-enhanced, cookie-cutter look. Women who look like the ones I grew up admiring (women like my grandmother, Helen Hayes, and Jessica Tandy) are nowhere to be found. Who's to blame for this? We all are. Magazines, billboards, TV shows, and movies are filled with images of preternaturally youthful, impossibly proportioned women.

We have a choice. We can buy into these images or we can make the conscious decision not to. True beauty isn't about looking like a supermodel (remember, they're freaks of nature) or a 20-something Barbie doll (what does the woman who created Barbie look like anyway?). True beauty is about accepting and feeling good about who you are. Here are some of the things to do as you approach your 50th birthday:

• Stop obsessing. Instead of obsessing over your "flaws" and the things you don't like about yourself, look at what's right. I can't tell you how many times women come to my makeup counter so fixated on the size and shape of one feature that they overlook everything else. When a woman asks me how to make her nose appear smaller, I point out her amazing smile and show her how to enhance her lips with the right lipstick and gloss. More often than not, she is pleasantly surprised by what she sees.

• Live in the present. We spend a lot of energy wanting to recapture what we used to look like, instead of appreciating where we currently are. I hated my arms when I was a teenager and often wore long-sleeved shirts. Now I look back on pictures from those days and I think that my arms looked just fine. I would have saved myself a lot of adolescent angst if I had made the best of what I had at the time.

• Be who you are. This means everything from learning to love the lines in your face to appreciating your own unique features. There's something incredibly beautiful about a woman with lines in her face, and I think we should start using the word 'living' instead of 'aging'. Facial lines are hard-earned proof that you've lived a rich, emotion-filled life. Take them all away and you would end up looking like a blank, plastic-faced mannequin. Tip: a little concealer and the right blush do wonders.

• Take charge of yourself. Instead of fighting the body you have, accept it and make the most out of it. Focus on being healthy, strong, and fit. Commit to making smart food choices and exercising regularly. Yes, this requires work and it's not a quick fix, but you'll look and feel better over the long term. I'm 47 years old and I'm still learning that there's a lot I can do to be the best version of myself there is.

We've all heard the adage "beauty is only skin deep." Well, it's high time we proved it wrong. Beauty goes far beyond the physical and what you see in the mirror. It begins from within and it's all about self-confidence. That's something that no doctor can prescribe. ☀

7

Put your best face forward

Just because you accept yourself doesn't mean you can't spruce up a few things. And now is a good time for a little nip-and-tuck prevention.

BY VALERIE J. ABLAZA, M.D., FACS

Ablaza is a partner in The Plastic Surgery Group in Montclair, NJ. She received her medical degree from The Medical College of Pennsylvania, completed her residency in plastic surgery at The New York Hospital/Cornell Medical Center, is a Fellow of The American College of Surgeons, and is a member of The American Society of Plastic Surgeons.

Have you recently walked past a mirror and thought you saw your mother's image out of the corner of your eye? Do you find yourself wearing turtlenecks more often? Is your TiVo set to Extreme Makeover, Dr. 90210, The Swan, or Nip/Tuck? Answer "yes" to any of these questions and maybe it's time to add "talk to cosmetic surgeon" to your To Do list. I often hear people say that they just want their external appearance to match the way they feel on the inside. And inside, they feel oh, about 30... not 50! That's my job: to help turn back the hands of time.

You might think those wrinkles, jowls, turkey neck, and extra inches have developed almost overnight, but I assure you the changes have been steadily, albeit slowly, since about your 35th birthday. The signs are subtle, but clear. Mornings when you look like you've pulled an all-nighter, even though you slept like a baby. People commenting on how angry you look all the time—when you're in a perfectly good mood. Love handles, droopy bellies and sagging thighs, even though you're the same weight you've been for the past 10 years. And breasts that have taken a decided slide southward!

I've also noticed a direct correlation between the amount of liquid make-up and concealer women use and how eager they are to get an appointment with me. It's that time of life when the same amount of make-up just doesn't give the same results. And witch hazel on cotton balls doesn't work for puffy eyelids like it did in college!

And men, don't think that you've completely dodged the curve ball. The aging changes in your face that have made you eligible for that "Most Distinguished Look" Award can also be refreshed with a number of cosmetic procedures. Take heart—there's even a solution for the love handles, spare tires and unwanted fatty deposits that have "suddenly appeared" in your breast area.

That's right. Cosmetic plastic surgery is not just for women. You may be surprised to know that men represent almost 20 percent of those opting for cosmetic procedures as a way to deal with image maintenance and change.

"Wait!" you're thinking. "I'm not old enough for plastic

surgery! Isn't that for really old people?" Hardly. After all, why wait until your face looks like melting wax before doing something about it? It's so much better to begin with subtle, relatively simple fixes today that will keep you looking good longer without dramatically altering your appearance. Think of such procedures more as a "make-better," and less as a "make-over." The goal of cosmetic procedures today isn't to turn you into someone else; it's to keep you looking just like yourself—only a younger, more refreshed, more relaxed version.

The old days when cosmetic plastic surgery was reserved for the very wealthy with lots of time on their hands are over. Today, anyone with a few hundred dollars can get a lunchtime facial peel, a Botox injection, or a quick laser procedure. Even a face-lift can be done in less time and with more natural looking results (no more "wind tunnel" effect) than in years past.

And the options. . . . Oh, there are so many for both men and women to enjoy!

How about an eyelid lift to remove excess skin and fat pockets on your upper and lower eyelids and raise the corners of your drooping eyes? A neck lift to restore a youthful jawline and improve the sagging angle of your neck? A facelift to not only tighten the skin on your face, but also to reposition sinking cheeks, minimize jowls, and give a boost to the corners of your mouth?

Happy with your face? Well, what about your chest, stomach, and thighs? Liposuction is great for removing unwanted fat on a man's chest as well as getting rid of excess fat from the abdomen, hips and thighs of both genders.

And if loose skin is the problem, tummies can be "tucked" and breasts and thighs can be "lifted." Push-up bras and girdles will become a distant memory. But you don't have to go the full surgical route. Botox not only minimizes forehead creases, crow's feet, and other wrinkles, but can also give a little lift to your eyebrows. Injectable materials including fat, Restylane, and Hylaform can fill in hollow areas and soften those hard-earned "character lines," while microdermabrasion, chemical peels, and laser resurfacing can help rejuvenate skin that had, maybe, a touch too much sun three decades ago.

How about permanent make-up to enhance fading lip color and avoid lipstick "bleeding" into the small vertical lines on the edges of your lips and corners of your mouth? And anyone who has become a victim of "short-arm syndrome" will appreciate not having to ever apply eyeliner or to pencil in thinning eyebrows again.

So if your spouse, significant other, friends or family members have run out of "perfect gifts" for your 50th birthday, drop a little hint for a gift certificate for a plastic surgery evaluation, or, even better, for a rejuvenation procedure. If they're not getting the hint, give yourself this perfect gift. There's nothing wrong with making changes to help you feel better about yourself!

8

Take your self back

Escaping the beauty trap isn't easy. You can regain the humor, intensity, and the balance you had in childhood. It's worth it!

BY ERICA JONG

Erica Jong is an award-winning poet, essayist, and best-selling novelist. She is the author of Fear of Flying, How to Save Your Own Life, Fanny: Being the True History of the Adventures of Fanny Hackabout-Jones, Parachutes & Kisses, Shylock's Daughter and Any Woman 's Blues, Inventing Memory: A Novel of Mothers and Daughters, among others. The following excerpt is from her best selling mid-life memoir Fear of Fifty (HarperCollins Publishers) published in 1994.

At fifty, the last thing I wanted was a public celebration. Three days before my birthday, I took off for a spa in the Berkshires with Molly (then thirteen) — slept in the same bed with her, giggling before sleep, slumber party style — worked out all day (as if I were a jock, not a couch potato), learned trendy low fat vegetarian recipes, had my blackheads expunged, my flab massaged, my muscles stretched, and thought about the second half of my life.

These thoughts alternated between terror and acceptance. Turning fifty, I thought, is like flying: hours of boredom, punctuated by moments of sheer terror.

When, on the evening of my birthday, my husband (who shares the same birthday but is one year older) arrived, I had to adjust to the disruption of my woman's world. He liked the food, but wisecracked about the holistic hokum. His critical-satirical male eye did not quite ruin my retreat, but somehow tainted it. I was doing inner work in the guide of outer exercise, and his presence made that inner work harder.

Real men don't like spas.

The year before, when he turned fifty, I had made a party for him. I sent out invitations that read:

He's fifty.

She's not.

Come help celebrate.

I still couldn't face fifty so I knew I did not want him to reciprocate for my fiftieth birthday. Nor did I want to do what Gloria Steinem had done: make a public benefit, raise money for women, and rise resplendent in an evening gown, shoulders dusted with glitter — as Gloria's lovely shoulders were — and say: "This is what fifty looks like".

Who can fail to admire such brave affirmation of older women? But I veered between wanting to change the date on my Who's Who entry and wanting to move to Vermont and take up organic gardening in drawstring pants and Birkenstocks.

I needed something private, female, and contemplative

to sort out these conflicting feelings. A spa was perfect. And my daughter was the perfect companion — despite her adolescent riffing that spares no one, her mother least of all. Still there is something about a woman turning fifty that is female work, mother-daughter work, not to be shared with the whole male world — or even with those representatives of it whom one loves and cherishes...

My husband and I have always made much of our birthday — in part because we share it, and because, having met in midlife, after the wreckage of many relationships, we treasure the synchronicity of our births...

...But fifty is different for a woman than it is for a man. Fifty is a more radical kind of passage to the other side of life and this was something we could not share. Let him make fun of "new age" contemplation. I needed it, as have women back to antiquity. Venus de Milo contemplates herself turning into the Venus of Willendorf — if she doesn't watch out.

You tell yourself you ought to be beyond vanity. You read feminist books and contemplate falling in love with Alice B. Toklas. But years of brainwashing are not so easy to forget. The beauty trap is deeper than you thought. It's not so much the external pressures as the internal ones that bind. You cannot imagine yourself middle-aged cute little you who always had "it" even when overweight...

...And then there are eternal questions of love and sex: Can there be friendship between men and women as long as the hormones rage and rule? How is sex related to love — and love to sex? Are we truly pigeonholed in our sexuality — or does society alone insist on this? What is "straight"?

What is "gay"? What is "bi"? And does any of it matter deep in one's soul? Shouldn't we get rid of these labels in an attempt to be really open to ourselves and to each other?

What was happening to me in the second part of my life? I was getting myself back and I liked that self. I was getting the humor, the intensity, the balance I had known in childhood. But I was getting it back with a dividend. Call it serenity. Call it wisdom. I knew what mattered and what did not. Love mattered. Instant orgasm did not...

Often I have tricked myself into writing with candor by telling myself I would not publish (or would publish only under a pseudonym perhaps even a male pseudonym). Later, I might be persuaded to sign the book by the loving letters I received from readers or by the publisher's need for a brand name. But during the writing process, I could be free, could knock the censor — my mother? My grandmother? — off my shoulder only by promising myself never to let my words see publication.

I wrote Fear of Flying that way and many subsequent books... Writing has often been accompanied by terror, silences, and then wild bursts of private laughter that suddenly make all the dread seem worthwhile.

But the great compensation for being fifty in a culture that is not kind to older women is that you are less about criticism and you are less afraid of confrontation. In a world not made for women, criticism and ridicule follow us all the days of our lives. Usually, they are indications that we are doing something right.

Is fifty too young to start an autobiography? Of course it is. But maybe eighty is too old.

Fifty is the time when time itself begins to seem short...At nineteen, at twenty-nine, at thirty-nine, even goddess help me — at forty-nine, I believed that a new man, a new love, a move, a change to another city, another country, would somehow change my inner life.

Not so now.

I know that my inner life is my own achievement whether there is a partner in my life or not. I know that another mad, passionate love affair would be only a temporary distraction — even if "temporary" means two or three years. I know that my soul is what I have to nurture and develop and, alone or with a partner, the problems of climbing your own mountain are not so very different.

In a relationship, you still require autonomy, separateness, privacy. Outside, you still need self-love and self-esteem.

I write this...from a place of self-acceptance, cleansing anger and raucous laughter. I am old enough to know that laughter, not anger, is the true revelation. I make the assumption that I am not so different from you.

Section Three

REDEFINING FITNESS

9

Limber up. Get flex-y with it.

Whether you're a couch potato or seasoned athlete, yoga can free your body in ways you never dreamed possible.

BY JONATHAN FIELDS

Jonathan Fields is the founder/director of Sonic Yoga, one of Manhattan's premier yoga centers, and the featured instructor in a series of nationally acclaimed yoga DVDs and videos. Jonathan is regularly featured in the media, including Self, Vogue, Elle, Fitness, Yoga Journal, Yoga International, Outside, Newsweek, The New York Times, and many more.

Feeling a little achy as you head toward the half-century mark? Waking up several times in the night? Having trouble falling asleep? How's your blood pressure? Stress level? Self-image? The wear and tear of the first 50 years of life on our bodies threatens to make the next 50 less than ideal.

But give me about three hours of your time a week, and I can guarantee you'll feel better.

No, it's not a pill, not a therapy, not a procedure. It's yoga, an ancient Eastern practice now being recognized as an outstanding adjunct to modern medicine in terms of keeping you fit, healthy, and centered.

If you're like most Americans, though, yoga conjures up visions of double-jointed 20somethings putting themselves into impossible positions and chanting. I've got news for you. Yoga today is about as mainstream as apple pie. Even small, rural communities sport yoga classes, and in large cities they're as ubiquitous as dry cleaners. Plus, given all those health benefits your doctor may even prescribe it for you!

So come along with me as I give you three user-friendly answers to three fairly giant questions: What is this thing called yoga? Why do I absolutely need it in my life? And, most important, how do I begin?

What is Yoga?

Asking a yoga teacher what yoga is a bit like asking a physicist what space is, but here's my best shot. Yoga is both a system of daily practices and a philosophy of living that originated some 5,000 years ago to liberate people from suffering and unify them with their true "selves" (a.k.a. "enlightenment"). Classically, enlightenment is the end to the yoga means.

The reality, though, is that most people begin yoga with the more accessible daily physical practices in search of simply feeling better, stronger, and calmer.

There are many different schools and styles of yoga, but all have certain common elements, including the use of postures, breathing exercises, and meditation. Postures are practiced to strengthen, cleanse, and heal the body. Breathing exercises deepen the cleansing effect and help balance energy in the body. And meditation is amazingly powerful at quieting the mind and bringing you back to center.

Why Do I Absolutely Need Yoga in My Life?

Yoga is the ultimate one-stop lifestyle solution!

It can help:

Reduce stress, and manage both depression and blood pressure.

Strengthen every muscle in your body.

Burn calories (certain styles of yoga) and manage or lose weight.

Improve your flexibility and ability to do more in life.

Promote good posture and decrease back pain.

Enhance concentration, clarity, and mental focus.

Improve balance, both on and off the mat.

Add something fun and joyous to your day.

Increase your confidence and creativity.

Sleep better and longer.

Provide a great community of friends.

OK, I Get It. How Do I Begin?

First, lose the excuse that you are too old, too tight, or too weak to do yoga. Strength and flexibility will come over time and, who knows, maybe you'll recapture a hint of youthful effervescence along the way!

The simplest way to start is with the postures. If you haven't exercised in some time, it's a good idea to check with your physician before beginning. Regardless of your level of fitness, starting with an introductory workshop or program that teaches the basic postures in an interactive format is a great idea.

Now, how do you choose your particular flavor of yoga? Here are brief descriptions of the major types:

Iyengar – High-level of attention to precision alignment, use of props, long holds. Best for those seeking therapeutic results or treatment of specific conditions.

Vinyasa/power yoga – Students "flow" from one pose to the next in a dance-like rhythm, tied to the breath. Dynamic and often challenging.

Ashtanga – Similar to vinyasa/power yoga, but usually refers to a specific, fixed sequence of very physical and dynamic postures that are held for a shorter time.

Restorative – Gentle, supported poses with lots of attention to individual needs. Good for those seeking a peaceful, accommodating practice or those recovering from injury or illness.

Hatha - Hatha is actually a term encompassing all of the physical practices, but these days it has largely come to signify a gentler, more centering approach to the practice of postures.

Anusara – Similar to Iyengar, emphasizes alignment and precision with a bit more flow.

Kundalini – Emphasizes breathwork, freestyle movement, and student interaction.

Integral – A gentle posture practice with strong grounding in breath, meditation, and study.

If it is within your means, working with a private teacher is a very powerful way to study. It allows for an experience completely tailored to your needs, abilities, and limitations. The best way to find a qualified private teacher is often through referrals and references. If you can't find a teacher through referrals, try the Yoga Alliance (YA) teacher registry at www.yogaalliance.org. While many great teachers on not registered with YA, it does provide a place to start.

For many of us, classes are a more realistic option. It's a great way to explore the many forms of yoga to see which type works best for you. It is always a good idea to begin with a gentle approach and then move to a more intense practice.

Chanting, in yoga, is not about religion, but about community and a universal sense of spirituality. Chanting can be very intimidating for people who are new to the practice. If you're not comfortable chanting, you may sit in silence or search out a class or teacher who doesn't chant. Before completely abandoning chanting, though, try sitting in silence and maybe joining in occasionally. I cannot tell you how many students have told me that they were terrified of chanting at first, but now love it.

Most importantly, as you begin your exploration, take a long-term perspective and move into it with a sense of humor and lightness. There may be stumbles along the path to a far more fulfilled place in your world. And, just as important, you will feel — physically and emotionally — much better!

Namaste ("The light in me honors the light in you")

10

Learn to bellydance

Let this beautiful Middle Eastern tradition — sexy, fierce, and energetic — help you fall in love with your 50 year-old body. In this dance, ripeness triumphs over beauty.

BY TaRESSA STOVALL

TaRessa Stovall is an author, mother, and, of course, a belly-dancer. She is co-editor of Proverbs for the People: Contemporary African-American Literature (Dafina/ Kensington, 2003), co-author of A Love Supreme: Real-Life Stories of Black Love (Warner, 2000), and author of The Buffalo Soldiers (Chelsea House, 1997). She is also a newspaper columnist, public relations consultant, and professor of public speaking.

This dance welcomes you to your 50s as no other. It does not demand special skills or talent; it does not require experience or reward one body type over another. Young, sleek bodies have no advantage over our riper, more mature bodies whose life stories are etched onto our curves. No one measures her neighbor's contours or dress size;

there is no reason to compare. This one thing — the bond of womanhood — binds you to the dance and fills you with its possibilities.

"It is a dance of women's power centers — the breasts, the belly and the hips," says my teacher, Kristen Radden, and all of these things, she emphasizes, are supposed to be full and round! You learn that fleshiness is not bad or revolting or sinful. You come to class and learn to swing what you were taught to suppress, and to relax what you've spent your life holding in. You move your body and it moves you and something deep within you shifts, realigns, and is healed.

The music starts and you begin to sway. Slowly at first, then you pick up the rhythm. Then the flow of the harmony. Each movement is gentle, yet precise. Energetic yet elegant. And ever so fabulously feminine in a very empowering way.

Your lower body is grounded in the energy of the earth. Your middle body mimics the rolling waves of oceans, lakes and rivers, the dancing flames of fire, and the sensuous swirls of smoke. Your upper body is like pure air — light and graceful as a breeze.

You feel connected to ancient women from around the world — women who danced as part of everyday life, to mark rites of passage, to express emotions that had no words. Women whose movement was prayer, meditation, and spiritual ritual. Your hips move in a circle as you retrace the pathways you have traveled from baby to girl to young woman to adult. From daughter/sister to mother/aunt/godmother/grandmother, from student to professional, from potential to possibility, from purpose to struggle to triumph to promise tested and fulfilled.

You dance to the cycles of your biological imprint: menstruation, pregnancy, birth, and menopause. You dance your biography to music swirling in unfamiliar rhythms, finding freedom in not knowing which way the sound will lead. Something in your body/memory connects to the DNA of your foremothers, and you find yourself performing ancient undulations of the pelvis, mimicking the traditional movements that women worldwide learned in preparation for childbirth.

The music carries you to distant lands as you imagine yourself an innocent womanchild, a sultry temptress, a nurturing lover, a warm mother, a fierce warrior, and an elegant queen just coming into the magic of your personal power.

I am woman! See me flow, see me circle, see me shimmy. I am earth mother, star-child, water maiden, and fire goddess. I am the carrier of life, the nurturer of the world, the beauty of the changing seasons reflected on my face and in my gently shifting curves. See my dance — as gently hopeful as the first sign of spring green; as sensual as the tempting heat of summer; as richly gorgeous as the falling leaves; as delicately breathtaking as the first, unspoiled snow.

You tie on a hip scarf and delight in the tinkling of coins or the swaying of fringe as you learn to shimmy — first slowly, then faster, then in a blur of movement that is almost always accompanied by spontaneous laughter. The little girl — the one who became obscured by the twists, turns, and challenges of growing up and fitting in and meeting expec-

tations and looking, behaving, and moving a certain way —
is liberated by the dance. She bursts forth from your heart,
where she has been waiting for you to find that "shake it to
the East, shake it to the West, shake it to the one that you
love the best" beat that frees small girls to dance with wild
and innocent abandon.

Women who have excelled at other forms of dance find
new challenges in belly dance, while some who have always
thought they had two left feet find the key to unlock their
natural rhythms, bodysong, and grace. You find that learning this exotic dance to the wildly undulating music is like
learning a new language with an unfamiliar alphabet. As
you work to master the basics, you find your mind, body,
and spirit striving to unite, for it is in this dance that they
will truly work as one. You learn that a dance form that has
been misunderstood as sexually bawdy and aggressively
brazen in the West is, in fact, subtle, elegant, tender, and
sensual in the most delicate and classy way. It makes you
feel, simply, lovely.

You are thrilled by the "dress-up" possibilities of the cos-
tuming — which is just as addictive as the actual dance!
Sumptuous fabrics in gorgeous riots of color invite you to
try on new selves and perhaps discover hidden aspects of
yourself in the process. The drape of the fabric conceals,
reveals, highlights, and shadows as you need it to. You find
yourself mesmerized by the bright jewelry, the alluring
makeup — none of which is required, but all of which offers
a world of expressive delights. Slipping on sets of finger
cymbals gives you access to new rhythms bursting forth from
your soul. You are musician and dancer at the same time,

moving to a personal interpretation of song.

My fellow dance enthusiasts are doctors, lawyers, accountants, full-time mothers, grandmothers, retirees, college students, military officers, arts administrators, secretaries, and entrepreneurs. None of that matters; once we encircle our hips in glowing fabric and raise our arms in supplication to the music, we are whoever we want to be, whichever combination of selves — real or imagined — suits our fancy at any given time.

We dance with the motion of love discovered, with the sway of a mother comforting a child, with the weight of heartbreak and the fragile promise of love reborn.

Each woman in this ageless, timeless dance is writing her biography, her truths, her questions and her quests, her sorrows and her triumphs, and the lessons she has learned. In a culture that tells us we are to look like young boys and work like hard-charging men, we relax into the woman-power of softness that embraces and revives us at every level. We eschew our labels, titles and categories to simply be.

And we shimmy with the sheer, wondrous pleasure of it all.

11

Sit still; meditation is medicinal

Meditation isn't just for the mind and spirit. It can also benefit your body.

BY ROBERT H. SCHNEIDER, M.D.

Robert H. Schneider, M.D., FACC is widely recognized as a leading authority in the area of alternative health, aging, and heart disease. He has testified before the White House Commission on Complementary and Alternative Medicine, and the US Congress' Prevention Coalition as well as consulted with health policy agencies and experts around the world. His book Total Heart Health: Your Complete Program to Prevent and Treat Heart Disease with Maharishi Consciousness Based Health Care, was published by Basic Health Publications in the fall of 2005.

We used to look forward to birthdays. Our 16th when we could drive; our 18th when we could vote; our 21st, when we graduated from college and truly became adults. Back then, we wanted to see our numbers increase.

But all too soon, increasing numbers were no longer something we looked forward to. And today, it seems, all the numbers are headed in the wrong direction: up. Blood pressure, cholesterol, weight, triglycerides, body fat. For most of us they keep creeping higher, always higher, along with our age. I suggest that you use the occasion of turning 50 as the impetus to start bringing those numbers down.

Before you get too frustrated, I have some good news. It's possible to reverse the numbers associated with aging — without medication! You simply need to sit and meditate for 20 minutes twice a day.

Yes, sitting quietly for 20 minutes relaxing your mind with Transcendental Meditation, or TM, the most studied form of meditation, can actually reverse the aging process. Over time, those numbers we talked about above, the ones used to determine your physiological age, are systematically reduced, even as your chronological age increases. Don't take my word for it; I have the studies to prove it – studies published in some of the top peer-reviewed physiological and medical journals in the world.

First, let's talk about what TM is — and is not.

Let me reassure you that it's not weird or difficult. You don't have to be into yoga or give up eating steak. You don't have to wear a robe. You don't have to be a New Age hippie. You don't even have to be convinced that it works.

TM technique is surprisingly simple and easy, as natural as falling asleep. In my medical practice and research I've introduced it to people of all ages from all walks of life. Everyone, regardless of culture, language, gender, ethnicity, philosophy, or religion, has readily taken to this simple practice that makes use of the natural tendency of our mind to settle down and doesn't require concentration or contemplation.

You sit quietly for 20 minutes in the morning and afternoon and use a mantra, or meaningless sound, to let your mind relax. You can do it anyplace, typically just sitting comfortably in a chair. Whether it's an airport or your living room, you just close your eyes and begin.

The key is to do it in a specific, effortless way. That's why it's necessary to learn the practice from a qualified teacher. Instruction takes about one-and-a-half hours a day for about a week.

What excites me is this: when you sit for 20 minutes, you're not just having a pleasant, relaxing experience. Your brain waves change, your blood chemistry changes, indeed, your whole physiology undergoes changes. Through TM, you have a unique way to gain deep rest in mind and body, which research shows actually stimulates the body's anti-aging repair mechanisms. But stick with TM; studies find it's distinctively effective when compared to other meditation techniques.

As a physician, this thrills me. Too often restoring health means men and women running around in white coats giving shots and pills, cutting people up, shocking their hearts, implanting devices. How wonderful to be able to offer something that isn't harmful or painful, and that can help in so many ways.

Much of our research has been with older folks, who are particularly susceptible to hypertension and heart disease. I love to see how they feel empowered when they learn the

TM program. Finally, they're not so dependent on somebody else doing something to them from the outside. They're helping themselves by tapping into their body's inner intelligence so it can heal itself. Often, as their numbers drop, they can even trash their blood pressure medication.

I want to see more of this. I want to see people around the world taking control of their own health. I envision a time when people age in a different way than they do now. What do I mean by this? Well, our research shows that people who meditate have a slower rate of physical decline than people who don't meditate.

In one study, for instance, people who had been practicing TM for more than five years were physiologically 12 years younger than their chronological age, as measured by a drop in blood pressure and improved vision and hearing. Even people who had been practicing TM for just a short time were physiologically five years younger than their chronological age.

Maybe you're asking yourself, "How can this be?" After all, all you're doing is sitting and letting your mind and body settle down. But we find that this pause triggers a host of changes. It's as if your body knows what it wants, and the deep rest for mind and body associated with TM enlivens your body's inner intelligence and gives it a chance to repair the damage associated with daily living.

My collaborators and I have looked at this self-repair mechanism particularly as it relates to cardiovascular disease. After practicing the technique for three months, the people we work with have an average decrease in blood pressure similar to what they'd have if they used medication. When we followed the progress of these older participants for up to 18 years, we found their death rates from heart disease decreased substantially.

Once we realized this, we began looking for the mechanisms: what changes are actually going on in the body that lower blood pressure in such magnitude?

When we reported what we found, it made news around the world. Turns out that the thickness of the carotid artery, which supplies blood to the head and neck, actually decreased after 12 weeks of TM. This is important because hypertension, or high blood pressure, results in hardening and thickening of the arteries (atherosclerosis), the cause of heart attacks and most strokes. Measuring the thickness of the carotid artery is a good way to measure this change.

Today, thanks in part to our studies, a growing number of medical professionals now recognize the benefits of meditation. Even medical textbooks and medical school classes typically mention its benefits, especially as they relate to heart disease.

The research in other areas is equally fascinating, especially for people like you, who are in middle age. Studies show, for example, that people who regularly practice TM have greater mental clarity and intelligence. Along with these changes in mind and body come changes in behavior. People who practice TM tend to be more harmonious and happier. And other studies find that the net effect of these changes in mind, body, and behavior can actually make a demonstrable positive change in society. In other words, a healthier, happier you has a positive effect on those around you.

So I suggest that you see turning 50 as an opportunity to take this new direction in revitalizing mind and body — and start reversing those numbers. ☀

Section Four

STAYING STRONG

12

Eat like a caveman

Travel backward in time to recapture the perfect diet. More fruit, less juice; less meat, more nuts.

BY FRED PESCATORE, M.D.

Fred Pescatore, M.D., is the author of a New York Times best-seller, The Hamptons Diet, that weds the health benefits of a Mediterranean-type diet with his strong belief in an opti-mized balanced nutritional approach. He is also the author of the top-selling books Thin For Good and The Allergy and Asthma Cure, as well as the top selling children's health book, Feed Your Kids Well.

I bet you're expecting some dull, boring dissertation about eating your spinach and never again spreading butter on your bread. Phooey! If I wrote that, you'd turn the page so fast you might rip it.

Instead, I've got another option for you when it comes to eating right (and losing weight without trying): Eat like a caveman.

Yup, you heard me right. If we all ate the way we're genetically programmed to — the way our great-great-great-

great (etc., etc.) grandparents ate, and lived, there'd be no need for diets, weight loss pills, or low-fat ice cream.

Just imagine what your ancestors' diet must have been like; they only ate foods they could catch, pick, or steal from other tribes. Aside from the threat of death from a rampaging mammoth, you can't get much healthier than that. This feast-or-famine lifestyle was imbedded in their genes; they hung onto every calorie they could find because they never knew where the next meal was coming from. Unfortunately, they've passed that "thrifty gene" down to us, even though we live in a culture where there's food everywhere we turn. So we continue to store fat for that day when we can't find any food. The best way around this? Eat like our ancestors did. This means:

1. Keep away from fast foods. That's right. Put the burger down and step slowly away. Although you may instinctively know this, how many of you still ate at a McDonald's this week? Even the healthier options in the drive-thru are nutritionally suspect. Some of the salads (particularly with dressing) often have more fat and calories than the burgers. After all, fast food to a caveperson was likely a raw root ripped from the ground – not a hunk of hard-earned meat.

2. Eat lean proteins. Your cave grandparents would only be able to catch wild animals, which are leaner than the meats we eat today. So stick with white meat chicken or turkey, pork, fish, and trim the fat from all red meats. Even better: try some game animals yourself. Buffalo, bison, elk,

venison — they're all lower in fat than the sirloin you might have had last night.

3. Load up on fruits and vegetables. Your cave relatives ate whatever grew in the ground or on trees, so the more of these you get, the better. Although today's dietary guidelines call for nine servings a day, research shows that upping the amount you eat by just one or two servings a day can significantly reduce your risk for disease. Potatoes, peas, corn, and other starchy vegetables don't count. Instead, make healthier choices like asparagus, broccoli, kale, spinach, and other dark leafy greens. As for fruits, choose those with the least amount of sugar, such as berries and melons, and try to avoid tropical fruits such as bananas (which contain 66 grams of sugar on average), mangoes, and pineapple.

4. Stick to whole grains. We've been eating these for 10,000 years. Then, about 100 years ago, refined grains (with all the fiber and nutrients stripped away) came into vogue. During the past 20 years, consumption of refined grains has skyrocketed and, not coincidentally, so have rates of obesity. So stick to fiber- and nutrient-filled brown rice, and whole grain breads and pasta. Make sure you read the labels: look for the word "whole" in the ingredient list.

5. Munch on nuts and seeds. Although demonized for several decades, the health benefits of consuming nuts can no longer be overlooked. They contain heart-healthy Omega-3 fatty acids, and studies show that the more you eat, the lower your risk for heart disease. Plus, snacking on nuts

can even help you lose weight. That's not permission to go crazy on the cashews, however. Stick to one ounce a day (about a handful) if you're trying to lose weight and two ounces per day otherwise. Also, choose healthy versions such as almonds, walnuts, and macadamias.

6. Avoid fruit juice. Our ancestors certainly didn't pluck a carton of orange juice off a tree; they ate an orange! Overall, fruit juice is only slightly healthier for you than soda and often has more calories. Studies find that the more fruit juice you drink, the fatter you're likely to be and the more likely you are to develop diabetes.

7. Pick the right fats. Although there are many oils available, science points towards monounsaturated fats as the healthiest ones. That means olive and macadamia nut oil. You can use olive oil for nearly everything except high-heat cooking. That's when macadamia nut oil, with its high smoke point, is the best choice. You also want to avoid trans fats. They're found in most processed foods, where they're used to make the items shelf stable. As little as three grams a day can significantly increase your risk for heart disease and stroke (an average donut has nine grams of trans fat). Lucky for us, beginning in 2006 you'll be able to learn if they're in your foods simply by reading labels. Until the new law takes effect, simply read ingredient lists and avoid foods that contain "partially hydrogenated" anything.

8. Pick local and seasonal foods. Isn't it kind of weird to be eating peaches in January? Not only is it more expensive,

but scientists are beginning to find that our bodies are best at absorbing nutrients locally grown, in season. Local can mean in your geographic area, not necessarily in your own backyard.

9.Go organic whenever possible. Sure, organic foods might cost a bit more and be harder to find, but they're worth it. They're not inundated with chemicals, and they contain trace mineral and natural antioxidants often missing in conventionally grown produce. Plus, the more organic foods we buy, the higher the demand will be, and the lower the price. And, of course, our ancestors only ate organic (OK, they didn't have a choice).

10. Learn to cook. It's not that hard. Spend a weekend cooking for the week ahead and all you have to do is reheat something at night. Much healthier than ordering in or driving through. And, unlike the cavemen, you have more options than throwing a hunk of meat on an open fire. To that end, make sure you also invest in the proper kitchen gadgets. No one would think of starting an exercise regimen without the proper equipment, so you shouldn't expect to live a more nutritionally sound life without the right preparation. Start with a good knife, a slow cooker (place everything you want to eat for dinner in the pot, go to work, and come home to a delicious meal) and an herb grinder.

Follow these few "rules" and you'll be eating like the cave dwellers in no time at all – and, in the end, you'll be healthier, thinner, and less prone to disease. After all, you've still got most of your life ahead of you — live it to the fullest! ☀

13

Take heart

While the rules for heart-health are different for men and women, there *are* rules. And they can save you from heart disease.

BY DAVID KATZ, M.D.

David L. Katz, M.D., is associate clinical professor of epidemiology and public health, director of medical studies in public health, and lecturer in medicine at the Yale University School of Medicine. In 2000, Dr. Katz founded, and now directs, the Integrative Medicine Center in Derby, CT.

D r. Katz has also published seven books, including the consumer health books The Way to Eat, and Cut Your Cholesterol. He recently co-authored his eighth book, a guide to daily health promotion practices entitled Stealth Health, now in press at Reader's Digest Books.

He also serves as the nutrition columnist for O, the Oprah Magazine, and in January 2005, Dr. Katz began a weekly nutrition column syndicated through The New York Times.

Perhaps men truly are from Mars and women from Venus. Certainly there are more than enough times when it feels as if we belong on separate planets. But while a woman's heart and a man's heart may beat to the tune of different drummers, both are sustained, or threatened, by the same vulnerable blood supply. If you subject either to stress, tobacco smoke, a sedentary lifestyle, poor nutrition, and/or obesity, we succumb quite comparably to heart disease.

Why care? Well, if you're 50, and you're interested in the next 50 years of your life, you had better. For heart disease is the leading killer of men and women in the United States. Yes, you heard right. Men and women. Actually, heart disease kills more than 10 times as many women as breast cancer; more women every year than all cancers put together, making it as much a woman's disease as a man's.

But enough of this. My mission is not to make you lament your susceptibilities, but to encourage you to exercise your power! Heart disease, in men and women, is eminently preventable. I want you to acknowledge your vulnerabilities not so you succumb to them, but so you recognize, confront, and conquer them. Veni, vidi, vici, and all that. You've come, you've seen, so let's conquer.

Heart disease is due to the accumulation of plaque, or "atherogenesis," in the coronary arteries, which can be caused by almost anything that damages blood vessel linings. It takes plaque years to accumulate to a dangerous degree, which is why our hearts may break in our youth, but they scarcely ever fail until we are a bit more, shall we say, mature.

That's not to say, however, that there aren't danger signs along the way. We call these "signs of cardiac risk." And while it would be great to have a single test that could tell you whether or not your risk for heart disease is elevated, we're just not there yet. Instead, we've got an array of important measures.

Let's start with blood pressure. High blood pressure can directly injure blood vessels by striking the inner lining with excessive force over and over again. You can just imagine the damage that causes! Ideally, your blood pressure should be below 120/80. And while there are numerous effective medications that can lower blood pressure if and when bona fide "hypertension" or high blood pressure develops, don't wait to find yourself on the wrong side of that line.

Lower your blood pressure and your risk of hypertension through physical activity, maintaining a healthy weight, limiting the amount of salt in your diet by steering clear of highly processed and fast foods, and getting plenty of health-promoting nutrients from fruits, vegetables, and grains.

Perhaps the best-known cardiac risk factor you can change is your cholesterol level. You know about cholesterol, right? It's a blood fat that travels throughout your blood and can build up in your arteries. Cholesterol is no longer a simple, single measurement, but is derived from several measures that comprise your "lipid panel." You want your LDL (that's the bad stuff), triglycerides, and total cholesterol to be relatively low, and your HDL (that's the good stuff) to be relatively high to minimize your heart disease risk.

The best way to get there? Eat only small amounts of saturated fat (found in red meat and full-fat dairy products) and trans fats (found in processed foods and often identified as "partially hydrogenated oil") while getting plenty of soluble fiber from oats, barley, beans, lentils, and fruit. Other ways to get there: cut out as much refined starch and simple sugars as possible (i.e., white bread, white rice, cakes, cookies, etc.) and make sure you're pursuing regular physical activity and working to maintain a healthy weight. Raising a glass can raise HDL, too; one alcoholic drink per day for women and up to two per day for men can be very good for your heart.

Oxidation can injure blood vessels and change cholesterol particles in ways that make it easier for them to gunk up your arteries. The real bad actor in atherogenesis is "oxidized LDL," a form of super bad cholesterol. You can minimize this form by filling your diet with antioxidants. It's not hard: just focus on vegetables, fruits, red wine, dark chocolate, and tea. I can only guess how pleased you were to find dark chocolate on that list!

All the functions needed to maintain healthy body tissues are also at work in blood vessels, and some measures of cardiac risk may indicate a problem with these functions. For instance, a high blood level of homocysteine, a certain kind of protein, suggests you're not getting enough B vitamins to help maintain and repair healthy tissues. The easiest way to get enough B vitamins is to take a good multivitamin/mineral supplement each day, particularly if you're 50 or older. If in doubt about which vitamin to choose, sign on to www.consumerlab.com for an objective appraisal of the choices.

Of course, there's more to a heart attack than just an accumulation of plaque. The plaque itself has to be soft enough to rupture. And blood platelets, special blood cells that help blood clot, need to be sticky enough to pile up at the rupture site and block the flow of blood through the damaged area. Once that blood flow with its life-carrying oxygen stops, you've got yourself a heart attack.

So the consistency of your plaque and the stickiness of your platelets are other signs of heart disease risk we can both measure and change. For instance, inflammation (the process that occurs when you injure yourself) tends to make plaque soft and vulnerable. One way to reduce inflammation is to eat fish, such as salmon, regularly. An even better bet is to take a daily fish oil supplement. Fish oil can also help make your platelets less sticky, as can Vitamin E. So, based on the evidence currently available, I recommend up to 200 IU of Vitamin E per day, but no more; if you're taking a good daily multivitamin, you're likely getting enough.

While there are many ways to measure cardiac risk, a few simple strategies serve to improve them all.

Don't smoke.

Engage in regular physical activity, accumulating at least 30 minutes of moderate exertion (i.e., you can still talk while you're exercising, but you probably can't sing) each day if possible.

Eat a balanced, prudent diet rich in vegetables, fruits, and whole grains.

Control your weight.

Limit your intake of processed foods (you'll easily reduce your sodium consumption and, most likely, your daily calories).

Control the stress in your life if possible, or at least your responses to it. If relaxing is not your long suit, consider yoga, meditation, or taking some classes in stress relief techniques.

Add to this regimen a multivitamin and a fish oil supplement, and your defenses are pretty robust. If you've done all this and you still have risk factors indicating a high risk of heart disease, that's the time to turn to medicine — but not before.

And remember: There are — or at least have been — entire cultures in which heart disease is virtually unknown. Not because the people don't have a genetic predisposition for heart disease, but because of the lifestyle they're leading. This implies that by applying what we already know, you can virtually eliminate your heart disease risk. The very heart of self-defense is in your hands.

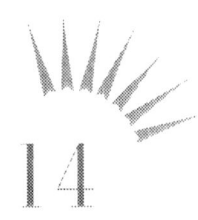

14

Bone up

Be good to your joints and bones now.
Be limber later.

BY MICHAEL R. WILSON, M.D.

Dr. Michael Wilson is a board-certified orthopaedic surgeon with over 25 years of experience. In 1993, Dr. Wilson entered practice at the Ochsner Clinic Foundation in New Orleans, a large, prestigious, multi-specialty organization similar to the Mayo Clinic. In addition to his busy surgical practice, he is Ochsner's orthopaedic residency program director, in charge of training 12 orthopaedic residents.

O K, let's get one thing straight: you don't just wake up at age 50 and suddenly notice those aches and pains. They've been creeping up on you, right? The question now is, what can you do about them today and what can you do to improve the likelihood that you won't be limping into the future?

First, it's important to understand that there are two separate issues here. One is the health of your joints; the other is the health of your bones. It's easy to get the two confused.

Even the terms we use for the illness of each — osteoarthritis for worn-out joints and osteoporosis for thinning of the bones — sound alike.

So let's start with a brief foray into the world of osteoarthritis, followed by my thoughts on osteoporosis.

I've probably spent more time in my career explaining what osteoarthritis is and isn't than in any other conversation with patients. Americans seem to think that arthritis is some sort of minor problem that, although irritating, should go away with Tylenol or Advil. In fact, osteoarthritis is a chronic, progressive, often crippling condition. It is the main reason orthopedic surgeons like myself perform over half a million total hip and knee replacements in this country every year.

Yet patients are often shocked and even disappointed to find out that what's wrong with them is "just arthritis."

"I'm in such pain!" they wail. "Don't try to tell me that it is just arthritis!"

Well, just arthritis is enough to force you to use a cane or crutches, keep you from sleeping, or steal your ability to walk from point A to point B. When it affects your hands, it can make the simplest activity either miserably painful or downright impossible. I see 50-year-old women who can't open a pill bottle and guys my age (54) who can't button a shirt. The preference of osteoarthritis for the spine, particularly the lower back, is one of the universal miseries of mankind and the most common reason Americans miss work or become permanently disabled.

I find it useful to understand end-stage osteoarthritis as organ failure in which the organ that fails is the joint. When your kidneys fail, you might go on dialysis. Eventually, if you're lucky, you get a kidney transplant. When your knee fails, it might be a slower process but in the end it can lead to total knee replacement — the orthopedic equivalent of a kidney transplant.

Osteoarthritis can result from damage, injury, or even inherited weakness in any of the structural components that work together to create a healthy joint. It is not just one disease but the common final outcome that results from many insults to the joint.

The big three symptoms of osteoarthritis are pain, swelling, and stiffness. They can occur in any combination and with any degree of severity from mildly limiting to incapacitating. It's fairly easy to diagnose arthritis with a physical examination and x-rays.

If you're like most 50-year-olds, you're ready at this point for the cure. Bad news — osteoarthritis can't be cured. So early on, the goal is to control your symptoms through exercise, simple medicines like acetaminophen (Tylenol), nonsteroidal anti-inflammatory drugs (NSAIDS) like ibuprofen, naproxen, or celecoxib (Celebrex), and the so-called "chondro-protective" (literally, "cartilage protecting") agents like glucosamine and chondroitin. As the disease progresses, these approaches may become less effective. Then, more aggressive surgical management, including joint replacement, may be necessary.

Notice I haven't said anything about diet. The only thing to know about diet and arthritis is that you should keep your weight within a normal range. Our joints are simply not designed to effectively support more than our ideal body weight.

As for glucosamine and chondroitin — well, it depends. They help some patients and have no effect on others. One thing I do know is that they do not rebuild cartilage. Nonetheless, many orthopaedic surgeons and rheumatologists I know take this stuff for their osteoarthritis, so that probably means something. My recommendation? Try a preparation that includes both for at least six weeks. If you feel better, keep taking it. If you don't, you're wasting your money.

If you do get to the point where you need a hip, knee, or shoulder replaced, you are looking at one of the most successful operations in the history of surgery æ 90 to 95% of all patients who have these surgeries end up with a good or excellent result. Although every major surgery has potential complications and none is without risk, I've seen joint replacement surgeries dramatically change my patients' lives, restoring function in a way that is nothing short of miraculous.

Now let's talk about thinning of the bones, or osteoporosis. Although this applies to women more than men, don't quit reading here, guys. Osteoporosis in men is doubly stealthy. It's overlooked in men just as it is in women because there are no symptoms at first; and it's ignored because we think of osteoporosis as almost purely a disease of women. Yet men have a greater risk of developing osteoporosis than prostate cancer!

Here's what's happening. We build up a certain amount of bone in our bone mineral bank by age 20 or so and then we either maintain it or spend it. We make deposits in the bone mineral bank by maintaining a dietary calcium intake of greater than 1500 mg a day and a vitamin D intake of 400 to 800 IU per day, and performing weight-bearing exercises such as walking, aerobics, tennis, or weight lifting. It's hard to get enough calcium in your diet to meet that requirement, however. So plan on taking a daily calcium supplement.

We make withdrawals via drinking diet soda, turning into a couch potato, smoking, drinking, and, if you're a woman, childbirth, breastfeeding, and the loss of estrogen that occurs with menopause.

The stakes are high. Osteoporosis leads to fractures — broken hips, compression fractures of the vertebrae, broken wrists and ankles. One in four women age 45 already has measurable osteoporosis, as do nine of 10 women over age 75. There are now over 300,000 hip fractures per year in the United States. As our Baby Boomer generation ages (that would be you), researchers estimate this figure will double by the year 2015. Here's how to keep from being part of that statistic.

Though the first step should be making the diagnosis of osteoporosis, all too often the first step is actually a mis-step, which results in a broken wrist or hip. The disease may have been silently progressing, your bones thinning slowly over the years, then bingo! A simple stumble results in a shattered wrist, shoulder, or ankle.

The gold standard to measure the strength of your bones, or bone mineral density (BM.D.), is the "DEXA" scan (Dual Electron X-ray Absorptiometry). Don't assume your doctor will consider this a routine part of your midlife physical exam and order it like a cholesterol level test, however. Unfortunately, even patients with fractures due to osteoporosis often don't get the BM.D. test they need. So don't be afraid to press your doctor for this.

Treatment for osteoporosis includes calcium, Vitamin D, and one or more of the newer drugs that actually can restore bone density, such as alendronate (Fosamax), risedronate (Actonel), and teriparatide, or synthetic parathyroid hormone (Forteo). Over time, these drugs may actually increase your bone mineral density, decreasing the rate and severity of fractures.

Then there's estrogen. The role of estrogen supplementation has become quite controversial lately, mostly because of much publicized studies from the Women's Health Initiative on its negative effects when it comes to heart disease and breast cancer.

Still, studies find that taking estrogen alone (without progesterone) can help prevent hip and spinal compression fractures in post-menopausal women. So talk to your doctor about whether estrogen therapy might be right for you.

In the end, the approaches to osteoporosis and osteoarthritis have some common features. At 50, you need to know where you stand. If a good physical exam, x-ray, or bone mineral density test shows you have or are starting to develop either condition, talk to your doctor about what you can do to minimize the effects. Not so ironically, similar lifestyle changes can make a big difference in the course of each: exercising regularly, keeping your weight down, watching what you eat, and avoiding injury.

15

Buff up your brain

No more jokes about "senior moments." Keeping your brain at its highest level is easier than you think.

BY BILL BECKWITH, PH.D.

Bill Beckwith, PhD, founder of Memory Management, Ft. Myers, Fla., has been helping people with their "senior moments" for more than 30 years, teaching at Ohio State University and the University of North Dakota. He also established the Center for Excellence in Memory Care, and served as clinical director of a major memory disorders clinic.

As I look into the mirror each morning, I know that I've changed. I don't look like I did when I was 30. The changes are obvious: My hair is gray, I have more wrinkles, and my skin has markings and blemishes it didn't have in my younger days. I don't always like these changes, but at least I can see them.

What are not so obvious are the changes that occur inside. For instance, I know that my bones aren't as dense as they once were; that my muscle strength and endurance have declined. I'm lucky; by living a healthy lifestyle these changes have been fairly minimal, and haven't caused any significant disability.

But what about my brain? Yup, your brain also changes as you age. Rather than weakening, like your muscles, it shrinks. In fact, your brain's potential peaks at age 2, when it contains the largest number of cells it will ever have. It's all downhill from there!

That doesn't mean your brain function has to go downhill. These days, we've learned a lot about what constitutes memory, what affects it, and what can be done to maintain it. Like an athlete who has to work out every day to stay in shape, you have to exercise your brain to maintain its health. But maintaining your memory goes beyond your brain; today we know that anything that affects the health of your body also affects the health of your brain. That means if you have high cholesterol, are overweight, smoke, have diabetes, eat an unhealthy diet, or don't get enough physical exercise your brain will suffer.

Suffer how? Well, by experiencing more of those memory blips that come as you age. You can't think of a word when you want; you have problems multitasking; you find yourself making inadvertent word substitutions, forgetting names, misplacing items. I'm not talking Alzheimer's disease here; I'm talking age-related memory loss.

And no, just because you may have already noticed some of these symptoms, it's never too late to slow the cycle. For another thing we've learned in recent years is that the brain is remarkably pliable, able to create new connections and new neural pathways to compensate for those that might have already been lost.

Start by stimulating your mind with mental exercise. Look at what you're currently doing for mental stimulation. If it's watching reality shows and reading People magazine, you're in trouble. You need to stretch your brain, continue learning, expose yourself to new experiences. These can be as minor as taking a new route to work every day and as major as returning to school for another degree. As simple as completing the daily crossword puzzle and as complex as learning a new language. How about a new hobby, like growing orchids, or collecting wine (new evidence showing moderate alcohol use can improve memory provides an additional incentive)?

Now take a look at your exercise program. Do you do some form of aerobic exercise for 40 minutes most days of the week? Do you have a resistance training routine? Both forms of exercise appear to uniquely contribute to mental efficiency. They also help your memory by helping you manage stress.

At the same time, you need to pay attention to what you're eating. Thanks to research over the past 20 years, we now know what kind of diet helps maintain a strong mind. That would be lots of fruit and vegetables. A minimum of saturated fats and salt. Regular servings of fish instead of red meat. And don't forget that glass of red wine.

Now, what if you've already noticed some of those age-related memory lapses? No problem, just follow a few clever tricks to help you over the rough spots. For example, learn how to use your calendar, really use your calendar. Too often, the only things on our calendar are those things we have to do. How about adding things we'd like to do, or simply need to remember? For instance, schedule in those 40 minutes of exercise each day. Schedule surprises for your spouse, like sending flowers or a card, calls to your mother, reminders to get the furnace checked, clean the filters, water the plants. There's no reason you have carry the minutia of everyday life around in your head; write it down!

Another external memory aid is to add things you need to remember to your daily routine. For instance, how do you remember to take your blood pressure medication (or multivitamin) consistently? Put the pill bottle in front of your toothbrush. Then it becomes part of an already-ingrained habit (I hope that brushing your teeth is a daily habit!).

Worried you'll forget important points of a conversation? Carry a small tape recorder with you to record these discussions (with the other person's OK, of course) so you can review them later and have a chance to reflect on them. For example, taking your tape recorder to physician visits will help you remember complicated information and medical directions (plus, your attorney will love it).

Always forgetting where your keys or wallet are? Create a take-away spot. Each evening, put the things you need for the next day next to the garage door (or whatever door you use to exit your house). Have a place for everything and put everything in its place. For instance, when you take off your glasses, always put them in the assigned spot, no matter how inconvenient, now matter how tired you are. I guarantee you won't forget where they are.

Right about now, you're thinking: He hasn't told me anything I don't already know. Of course! A healthy mind is all a matter of common sense. Follow these simple tips and you'll find that aging is not a disease to be avoided, but a journey of personal growth. With these steps, you can travel to the end of the journey with your memory and mind intact. ☀

16

Stop squinting

There are safe and simple ways to ward off bifocals and help you see your future clearly.

BY BRIAN S. BOXER WACHLER, M.D.

Wachler is the founding director of the Boxer Wachler Vision Institute in Beverly Hills, California. The former director of the UCLA Laser Refractive Center at the Jules Stein Eye Institute in Los Angeles, he has pioneered surgical techniques and guidelines that have become the industry standard, and serves as an investigator for numerous FDA clinical trials.

How do you know you're turning 50? When a friend or spouse says to you with a little grin, "This is a big birthday for you . . . let's have a party with all your friends," then hands you an invitation you can't read because you left your reading glasses at the office. Losing your ability to read anything, anywhere, without special equipment can be as mortifying as knowing that the AARP membership application is just around the corner.

This decline in your reading vision is called presbyopia, which means "aging eyes." It's an awful name, isn't it? So, if you don't mind, I've come up with my own translation: maturing eyes, which lends a certain grace to the process. After all, just think how much better it would have sounded if, when you first began having trouble seeing up close in your 40s, your eye doctor told you, "No need to worry, you've got the condition known as 'maturing eyes,' that's all." Somehow, that might have lessened the blow. In fact, you might have peered into the mirror and enthusiastically said to yourself, "I really do look more mature!"

While maturing eyes are largely unavoidable, you can take comfort in numbers. It's been a human condition ever since we made it past age 40 thousands of years ago. Of course, some greats in history were able to bypass the maturing eyes condition. Take Wolfgang Amadeus Mozart. He avoided maturing eyes not because his musical genius flowed over into his eyesight; but because he died at the age of 34 (before presbyopia hit).

So, when you consider the alternative, a few pairs of reading glasses don't seem like a huge price to pay for good sight.

In the past, that was the only option people with presbyopia had. Incredibly organized individuals stashed pairs all over their house, office, car, etc, buying them in bulk like diapers. Some tried to make the best of the situation with designer frames, refusing to be caught with a "granny glasses chain" around the neck. But there was no hiding it: they were still wearing reading glasses.

Today, however, those of us of a certain age are in luck: we have other options that may decrease our need for reading glasses. For instance, today there are bifocal contact lenses especially for reading vision.

If you're willing to go the surgical route, there are also minimally invasive vision correction procedures like LASIK, LTK, and CK that can help with presbyopia. You're probably familiar with at least the first in that alphabet soup of laser surgeries: LASIK. In this procedure, a tiny flap is created in the cornea (the outer windshield part of the eye) and a laser used to reshape the eye to focus your vision. LASIK for reading vision is most often used when your distance vision has also declined.

In LTK and CK, the doctor uses either laser energy (LTK) or radiofrequency energy (CK) to heat spots on your cornea to refocus your vision. Each is best for patients who still have very good distance vision, but for whom close vision, i.e., reading, is the only problem.

Not everyone will be a good candidate for reading vision contact lenses, LASIK, LTK or CK. Still, you'll never know until you ask! If you're interested, ask your eye doctor to evaluate you and discuss these options.

But have realistic expectations. Even though these techniques can significantly reduce your need for reading glasses, there is still no "silver bullet" that will give you perfect vision all the time without occasionally whipping out those extra spectacles.

That may change in the future, however. Researchers, including myself, are working on some exciting new procedures, such as implants placed inside the eye that allow your reading muscles to work again, which may vanquish the need for reading glasses forever.

Symptoms of maturing eyes do not stop with affected

reading vision, however. Also watch out for "dry eye syndrome," a burning, aching, gritty feeling in your eyes. It can hit first thing in the morning, leaving you with red eyes for the rest of the day or, if you wear contact lenses, force you to switch over to glasses.

The good news is that dry eyes can be treated with over-the-counter artificial teardrops. Also, swallowing a teaspoon of flaxseed oil or three flaxseed oil capsules a day can work wonders, not only for your eyes, but for your dry skin, too! Nonetheless, see your eye doctor to make sure nothing more serious is going on.

In fact, that's about the best advice I can give you as you hit the half-century mark: see your eye doctor, whether ophthalmologist or optometrist, for a thorough eye exam every year. Be sure your doctor checks for "quiet" diseases that might be brewing such as glaucoma, cataracts, and early signs of macular degeneration. This is also a good time to discuss options to make your mature eyes less "mature." Then, maybe, by the time your next big birthday rolls around, those reading glasses will be a distant memory. ☀

17

Look within: get a colonoscopy

Okay, it's nasty. But all you need to get through this life-saving rite of passage is a sense of humor.

BY PATRICIA L. RAYMOND, M.D.

Patricia Raymond, M.D., FACP, FACG, 44, takes medicine seriously . . .and herself lightly. She has taught thousands of medical caregivers to regain their passion for their medical careers through her company, Rx For Sanity (RxForSanity.com). Her story on the medicinal power of words entitled "Strong Medicine" appears in the book, Chicken Soup for The Caregivers Soul.

The author of Don't Jettison Medicine and the colonoscopy joke anthology Colonoscopy: It'll Crack U Up!, she is a frequent contributor to and editorial board member of Family Doctor:The Magazine That Makes Housecalls. Dr. Raymond also hosts House Calls, a weekly medical show on southeastern Virginia's NPR affiliate WHRO.

I figured out early on that the only way to get the horrified look off people's faces when I told them what I do for a living (I'm a gastroenterologist) is to poke fun at what I do and who I am. So I frequently introduce myself as a "Butt Meddler" or a "Big Buttinski." Which is why I feel qualified and, indeed, allowed, to give you a particularly personal, some might even say intimate, message as you enter your 50th year: Get a colonoscopy now!

You think I'm going to harp on the medical reasons for colonoscopy, don't you? About how 40% of 40-year-olds have one or more polyps æ little, fleshy, mushroom-like growths æ sprouting in their colon. About how, over a 10- to 12-year span, these polyps turn into cancer in about six out of 100 individuals. About how, as the second leading cause of cancer death, colon cancer is not to be taken lightly. And about how, given all these reasons, you need a colonoscopy now to look for and remove those polyps.

Naaahhhh. Too easy. Instead, I'm going to tweak two of your darkest desires: greed and the quest for fame.

"Greed?" you echo excitedly, spittle forming at the corners of your mouth. "A colonoscopy can make me rich?"

Sure. Just consider the late great Italian artist Piero Manzoni. If you didn't have your finger on the pulse of the 1960s pop art movement, you might not be familiar with Sig. Manzoni's BM art. In 1961, he canned his solid excretory material in some 90 tins. These exclusive exhibits were sold to art collectors when they were hot (pun intended) at peak poop prices as high as $75,000. Even today, prices remain steep for a Manzoni tin; in June 2002, the respected Tate Gallery in London purchased tin No. 04 for about

$38,000. Beyond the artistic value of the tins, however, there's another reason for the high prices: they're becoming increasingly rare. Seems that as time passes, half of the canned art has exploded.

Given that you can expect to expel about seven pounds of "debris" during your pre-colonoscopy cleansing prep, with careful collection and skillful marketing you, too, could hit the mother lode. An added bonus: transient weight loss. You may be able to fit into those "thin" jeans in the back of your closet!

Now, about that shot at fame (and I'm not just talking about the glare of our internal spotlight on your colon). While our generation is enthralled with buttocks (from the rounded slopes of J-Lo to South Park's Cartman and his adventures with the alien anal probe) our modern stars are nothing compared to the artistry of the great Petomaine, a Frenchman who was a sensation in Western Europe in the late 1800s.

A headline performer at the famed Moulin Rouge, Petomaine was known for his anal imitations and his ability to play wind instruments with his rectal control. Yes, this fartist was also a flautist. His legacy has not faded into oblivion, however. Now on the scene one may find an English former train conductor, stage name Mr. Methane, making a tidy living with what he calls "Controlled Anal Voicing."

What does this have to do with a colonoscopy? Well, any gastroenterologist will be happy to provide you with an opportunity to entertain the post-op crowd with controlled anal voicing as you expel the gas after your colonoscopy.

In all seriousness, however (and I take colon cancer very seriously), a colonoscopy is not nearly as nasty as it sounds. Here's how it works: First we flush you out, a universally disliked bit of extreme house cleaning. Then, after you check in and receive your IV and some really great drugs, we skillfully advance a flexible lighted endoscope around your colon (where, regardless of what your spouse or coworkers say, we rarely find your head).

We then inflate your colon with air to inspect the lining. If we find polyps, we snip them on our way out . . . as simple as that. The part with the hose only takes about 20 minutes — the whole shebang with check-in and recovery lasts about two hours. If don't find any polyps, we'll stop nagging you for 10 years; if we remove a polyp or you have a close relative with colon cancer, we'll see you back for a repeat personal periscopic party in five years.

The key is having fun while you're doing it. For instance, I encourage my patients to decorate their bottoms to celebrate various holidays that fall on or near their scheduled colonoscopy. Over the years, I've been greeted with hearts, pumpkins and black cats, even an American flag or two. Just imagine my surprise when I pulled back the sheet covering an elderly lady on Abraham Lincoln's birthday and found a miniaturized version (oh, the wonder of computers) of the Gettysburg Address taped to one lower cheek.

What can be done "by the people and for the people" if you do have a polyp? Don't panic. First, wait for the pathology report on your polyp. Many polyps are benign, meaning they're not ever going to turn cancerous. If you do grow the premalignant kind (called "adenomas"), a healthy diet full of fruits and vegetables and low in animal fat, vigorous exercise, high calcium intake, and a daily baby aspirin — all the things you know you should be doing anyway — will reduce your odds of growing more.

So get off your butt and get your colonoscopy scheduled today! ☀

Section Five

MANAGING YOUR CAREER
AT MIDLIFE

18

Re-appraise yourself

**In your 50s, you're more valuable to your employer
than you realize. But it's up to you to show them
what you're worth.**

BY MARY FURLONG

Mary is the President of Mary Furlong & Associates. For 20
years, she has guided the digital marketing strategies of major
U.S. corporations for their 45+ age markets. She has served
as an advisor to the President and Congress during the
Clinton Administration, and a member of the New Zealand
Investment advisory board. She is a member of the Business
Forum of the American Society on Aging. Mary has appeared
on CBS, the Today Show, PBS, and NPR to discuss issues
related to trends in aging and technology. Time Magazine
recognized her contribution as chairman of ThirdAge Media
by honoring her in 1999 as one of its "Digital 50." In March
2001, Fortune Small Business Magazine named Mary as one
of the "Top 25 Women Entrepreneurs."

There is an old joke that says the closest most people
come to perfection is on an employment application.
Even if that's true, career professionals just turning age

50 might be the next best example of perfection, at least when it comes to job productivity.

How's that, you say? How can a 50-year-old bring more to the table than an up-and-coming 25-year-old or seasoned or savvy 37-year-old just hitting his or her stride?

I think it's a no-brainer. Older workers bring a plethora of benefits to the workplace that younger workers can't. Take intellectual knowledge. Older workers have more of it, having spent more years honing their craft and getting to know their industry and their company.

Or how about leadership and, by extension, mentorship? More experienced workers in their 50s often set the tone for professionalism and leadership in the workplace. They've seen it all, faced just about every challenge, and are rarely surprised by events, both good and bad, that arise in the workplace. After all, there is a lot to be said for a steady, calm hand on the corporate steering wheel in times of crisis. Fifty-something workers possess such attributes in spades.

Unfortunately, older workers still face something of a stigma in the workplace and in their careers. "The end is in sight", critics say. "He/She is a great worker and valuable contributor, but might be getting a bit long in the tooth. Maybe we should bring in someone younger . . . and cheaper."

Okay, you won't find any management types uttering those words publicly, but you just know that the sentiment is out there. Out with the old and in with the new, and all that.

How can 50-something workers fight back against this "soft" bias against older workers? Simple. By showing management that you still possess a great deal of value and, by virtue of your deep experience, superior leadership skills, and vast industry knowledge, you are indeed irreplaceable.

What makes an invaluable, irreplaceable 50-something worker? I maintain that it's a worker who combines the attributes of attitude, ambition, enthusiasm, integrity, determination, discipline, and work ethics to become a lean, mean, career-advancing machine – even at age 50. They still contribute across the board and are not easily pigeonholed by age, gender, ethnicity, or any other demographic a pointy-headed academic can roll out. What makes them stand out in a crowd is their record of achievement in their careers and the smiles on their faces owed to the fact that they're doing what they love to do.

"Hey," you might say reading this. "I have all those attributes, but nobody's calling me irreplaceable". But success transcends simply having the tools to succeed. Irreplaceable professionals are those career professionals who take these attributes and use them creatively. Here are some examples:

An irreplaceable 50-something career professional is someone who . . .

. . . Still actively seeks to get ahead

For example, a good 50-something career professional invariably asks if there's anything he or she can do to help the company. In effect, the worker is asking, "How can I make a larger contribution?" It's contributions that make successful careers, especially in the long run. Good 50-something professionals are never passive. That's why they are promoted, and then promoted again. Even at age 50.

. . . Knows the lay of the land

More seasoned workers know how their workplaces operate. They've figured out whether most promotions are based on creativity or attention to detail, sales or produc-tion/operations experience, computer or interpersonal skills. Then they work on the skills needed to capitalize on their workplace's culture.

. . . Creates opportunities – and takes responsibility

Ideas are the lifeblood of the workplace. Consequently, 50-something workers constantly deliver well-researched ideas and then volunteer to take charge of their execution. Initiative is another way of saying you deserve to continue to succeed in your career.

. . . Become experts in their field

Yogi Berra once said that you can learn a lot by watch-ing. True enough. Watch and listen long enough and you could soon become an expert in your field. And nobody does that better than a 50-something career professional. Rather than sitting and waiting for someone to come along and proclaim them an expert, as too many workplace denizens do, these workers have long since learned go out and become such an expert. Whether it's taking a class to learn Excel, offering to write for an industry trade magazine, or even offering to talk in front of a Chamber of Commerce Group, 50-somethings won't hesitate – and more important aren't afraid – to become industry experts. Imagine giving a speech on manufacturing line innovations and noticing your CEO was in the audience? Becoming an expert is hard work for younger professionals – they don't have that same "lay of the land" knowledge that you do. Take advantage of that.

. . . Treats their careers as their own small business

Older workers have learned over the years how to take control of their own careers. They don't like leaving things to chance and possibly seeing someone else take control of their workplace reputations. Like the neighborhood grocer or that software startup out by the interstate, a 50-something career professional takes reputation and responsibilities personally. Remember, thinking like a small business owner enables you to react fast to problems. And there's no greater value to a company than someone who solves problems fast.

. . . Knows their industry cold

A more experienced professional can just about cite chapter and verse on what their industry is up to on a daily basis. That sounds tough, especially for ultra-busy people like single parents or professionals who volunteer in their community. But all becoming savvy about your industry entails is reading the industry newsletter, checking out "The Wall Street Journal" or "Business Week" or the industry trade publications that are invariably laying about the workplace. Even better is developing your own contacts in the industry and chatting them up once a week or so. The Web is a big help, too. Industry associations almost always have Web sites chock full of information and data on your business. Or, subscribe to an online "clipping" service that will e-mail you news and information on your business community. Lexus-Nexis (www.lexusnexus.com) and Northern Light (www.northernlight.com) are good places to start. So are Business Wire (www.businesswire.com) and PR Newswire (www.prnewswire.com). Take advantage of these resources.

. . . Knows the value of being a mentor

Invariably, a younger worker lines herself up with someone who can champion her progress inside the executive boardrooms. In a smaller business that may be the CEO or the office administrator. In larger businesses a mentor can be the director of your department – or another department – or simply a fellow co-worker who's got the ear of company decision makers. In virtually all cases, that mentor is an older worker willing to share his or her knowledge and experience for younger protégés. Management loves mentors - - shared knowledge means a more savvy workplace. That usually translates into larger profits and a successful company.

. . . Has developed a fat Rolodex

Collecting business cards might seem like a waste of time to some people. But a more experienced worker knows that a phone number here or an e-mail address there can come in handy down the road. If you're attending a conference and don't have your business cards to hand out, or don't work hard to hand them out, you might be missing out on a bigger and better opportunity down the road. Contacts also come in handy when looking for good information on your industry. While nobody likes a pest, one thing I've learned in business is that people love to talk if you give them a chance.

. . . Stays ahead of the education curve

Let's face it. We're in a global economy now where information is as much a commodity as compact disks or convertibles. As technology changes seemingly on a daily basis, it's the savvy 50-something worker who keeps up. That could mean taking that class in Web design or simply chatting up your co-workers for the latest trends in commerce and technology. Think of it as business insurance.

. . . Recognizes what they are worth

A successful 50-something professional always knows his or her value to their company, to their industry, and to potential future employers in myriad industries. There's no shortage of surveys and annual reports on salaries in the workplace. Check them out and see where someone of your experience and position stand. Another good idea is to scout out the help wanted ads (many include salary ranges these days) or contact an employment recruiter who's been around the block. Such a person can tell you what you're worth on the open market.

Becoming Indispensable

There are other, more humanistic ways that separate seasoned older workers from the rest of the pack. They seem to know who they are and how to relate to others. They know how to play office politics (more importantly they know they HAVE to play office politics to get ahead) and know how to communicate with everyone in the workplace, from the intern in the mailroom to the company president.

Plus they take workplace issues in stride. They know how to find something positive in every negative experience. Rather than feeling victimized over the fact that they didn't get that promotion, they focus on what they can learn from the situation. They may find that they need to brush up on their interview skills or polish their resume in preparation for a new job search – even at age 50, if need be. In that way, even their disappointments become a stepping stone, not a roadblock.

Like fine wine, the best career professionals are the ones who age gracefully. So it goes with the 50-something worker.

19

Stay curious, be relevant, and THRIVE!

**Sometimes, success locks people into ruts.
Three artists offer advice about how to remain
inspired after 50.**

BY DAVID EBONY

David Ebony is associate managing editor of Art in America
magazine. His most recent book, Carlo Maria Mariani, was
published by Volker Huber, Frankfurt, 2002.

The best artists inspire. That is, after all, part of their job.
They give us new ideas, new ideals and, in some cases,
a new sense of humor. Recently, when facing the dis-
tress of recently turning 50, I looked to artists in my age
bracket for hope and inspiration. Maybe they could help me
deal with the daunting uncertainties of middle age. I found
the promise of renewal, and more, in the stories of three of
today's most prominent and influential artists: Cindy
Sherman, Fred Wilson, and Ross Bleckner. The photo-artist,
the sculptor/installation artist, and the painter, respectively,

are thriving, not merely surviving, as they settle into their 50s. All three are already internationally renowned for the sizable contributions they have made to contemporary art. Yet these innovators continue to explore a broad array of technical experimentation in their art, and touch upon a wide range of issues and themes, including identity, race, and sexuality. Today, they are at the pinnacle of their creative powers.

Photo-artist Cindy Sherman, who turned 50 in 2004, maintains a positive, inquisitive, and unassuming attitude about herself, her work, and her surroundings, which might seem unlikely for one who has been in the glaring and often unforgiving art-world spotlight for more than 20 years. She's confident and fearless enough to submerge her good looks further than ever in her most recent work, a stunning series of self-portraits in which she assumes the guises of outrageous and sometimes grotesque clowns. These colorful, large-scale images met with considerable acclaim in exhibitions in New York and London.

In pondering the notion of turning 50, Sherman doesn't look back. She has no interest in resting on her laurels, despite an extraordinarily successful career æ one of those rare coincidences of critical respect and commercial appreciation (her works regularly sell in the six figures these days).

"I don't ever want to repeat myself. I can't be bored. I'd rather be apprehensive and unsure of what I'm doing in order to challenge myself."

She has myriad ambitions for her work. A one-time Hollywood film director (Office Killer, 1998), she says, "I'd still like to write a script and direct another film of some sort, although it doesn't have to be feature length. I've been thinking of making some sculptural pieces, too, ever since I did sets for a dancer friend last year. I'd like to become more adept at using Photoshop [a computer program for artists and photographers] for fun and for work. I'm open to using it more in my work, but I'm just not sure how, except for backgrounds right now.

"I want to travel more, for fun rather than for work, and I'd like to get back to learning to play the piano."

Bumping into Fred Wilson during a gala opening of the new Museum of Modern Art in the fall of 2004, I brought up the question of his milestone birthday and his inclusion in this book. "I'm not sure how to respond. Now everyone will know I've turned 50!" He needn't worry. With his vivacious demeanor and dashing good looks æ complete with stylish dreadlocks and mischievous, piercing eyes æ he's obviously hit that magic number in exemplary style. And his career could not possibly be going better. Recently, he has received a great deal of attention for his elegant and penetrating installations, sculptures, and two-dimensional works.

In 2003, Wilson represented the United States at the ever-prestigious Venice Biennale. Appearing shortly after the U.S. invasion of Iraq, his sumptuous and generous presentation of large-scale sculptures, photo pieces, and installations, which filled the American pavilion, was a subtle-yet-impassioned plea for justice and tolerance. It was one of the Biennale's more thoughtful and profound displays. It focused on important racial issues, both in general terms and with regard to Italy's assimilation of African immi-grants. And, as if attaining that career goal was not enough to sustain him, an extensive museum survey of his work, "Objects and Installations, 1979-2000," recently toured the U.S., appearing in eight major venues. During his 50th birthday year, the highly acclaimed show was on view at the Studio Museum of Harlem in New York, his hometown.

Ross Bleckner, born in 1949, remains one of the most charismatic personalities in the New York art scene. He embodies the notion that the 50s can be among the best and most fulfilling years of one's life. Over the years, he has contributed, by means of his expansive and elegiac can-vases, a uniquely humanistic meditation on the AIDS crisis. He continues to paint haunting, macrocosmic and micro-cosmic images of ethereal spaces. Building upon his well-known vocabulary of forms, including birds, candles, and urns, his recent compositions feature clusters of blood-cell shapes, which address metaphysical concerns of the body, life, love, death, and transcendence. These have been featured in several recent well-received (and sold-out) shows at home and abroad.

Bleckner, usually surrounded by a posse of attractive young admirers, is at the top of his game. "In regards to being in my 50s, I feel grateful to be here and to be comfort-able with myself and in good health. I aim to keep focused, accept limitations and keep things simple, or even simpler. It's important to be engaged with the world outside of myself yet stay in my own rhythm, no matter what. Not to become an 'older artist' is key. I want to stay curious and to be relevant. To be a person who can be happy a lot of the time without thinking that being happy is what it's all about. Getting over yourself already makes one happy. Make some kind of peace with yourself. Calm, focused and clear is the new happy. Welcome to 50, the new 40."

Spending time with these talented artists help me find a new sense of hope, as all three are, as they settle into their 50s, at the peak of their professional and creative lives. ☀

20

Hire yourself

If you're passionate, competent, and have a good plan, 50-plus is an ideal time to start your own business.

BY ALAN WEISS

Alan Weiss is one of those rare people who can say he is a consultant, speaker and author and mean it. His consulting firm, Summit Consulting Group, Inc. has attracted clients such as Merck, Hewlett-Packard, GE, Mercedes-Benz, State Street Corporation, Times Mirror Group, The Federal Reserve, The New York Times, Avon, and over 400 other leading organizations.

His has published over 500 articles and 23 books, including his best-seller, Million Dollar Consulting (from McGraw-Hill). His newest books are Organizational Development (John Wiley & Sons) and Life Balance: How to Convert Professional Success Into Personal Happiness (Jossey-Bass/Pfeiffer).

In my line of business, entrepreneurs have always led the pack. And these days, there is no shortage of like-minded go-getters. More and more people are starting businesses at

116

ages traditionally seen as the beginning of retirement, or starting down entirely new career paths.

Whether your reasons are downsizing, early retirement, disgust with others controlling your destiny, or a passion for a particular pursuit, there are some absolute imperatives required to succeed. So, no matter what your motivation, here are the "musts":

First, there must be a defined market for your services. That market may be pre-existing (sales or business organization); it may be created (the Walkman® led to the IPod®, and no one knew they would ever need such a device); or anticipated (the need to manage virtual team members who never see other and are geographically diverse). But you must define what need you are addressing or anticipating.

Second, you must have the competency not only to meet the need, but also to compete well against others who already do. That means that a hobby or avocation isn't enough unless you're truly distinctive in your approach, methodology, technology, and so forth. Starting a business to repair toy trains won't work if you're merely a dabbler and not an excellent electrician and metalworker. Similarly, beginning a sales consulting operation will not be very effective if you are a good sales person but have never been a sales trainer.

Third, you must have passion. Make no mistake; no matter the nature of your new enterprise, you're in the marketing business too. You have to sell yourself and your business, and there will be a ton of rejection. Passion for your pursuit and your value will help overcome the inevitable disappointments and detours.

At 50+ you have an unusual advantage, in that you probably have a wealth of experience to draw upon, have made most of your mistakes long ago, and have a great network and/or contact list. These are distinct advantages of "maturity." (The playwright Tom Stoppard observed that, "Age is such a high price to pay for maturity.")

And that brings us to the next step: Contact everyone you know. That's right, everyone. Make a list of friends, acquaintances, former colleagues, customers, vendors, professional associates, civic group contacts, etc. Send every one of them an email, a voice mail, or a conventional letter stating what you're now doing and asking if you can be of assistance to them and/or whether they can give you the names of people you might be able to assist. Networking is Job One. If you don't tell them, they won't know you're there or what you're doing. If you don't blow your own horn, there is no music.

In order to get your business off the ground, you'll need to develop a business plan (to give you a blueprint to follow for your business) and a marketing plan (to attract customers) for your new business. A good business plan should explain what your business does, how duties are delegated, and how you are going to make money. Pretty standard stuff.

Marketing plans are different. If you're not sure how to

create one, then just answer these three questions:

1. What is the value proposition you bring to market, expressed as a business outcome? (For example, training classes are not value propositions, but increased sales at lower cost of acquisition are.)

2. Who is the likely buyer who can actually write a check for that value? (It's probably not a training manager, but may well be the vice president of sales, which means that's the person to talk to.)

3. How do you reach and market to that buyer?

You should also invest in the following:

• Quality letterhead, business cards, and envelopes

• A presentation folder and promotional material ("position papers," biographical sketches, references, typical client results, an array of services offered, etc.).

• A top-line computer and printer.

• A reliable cell phone and multi-line office phone.

• A very well-made suit that you wear only to new prospect meetings.

• Subscriptions to relevant literature (e.g., The Wall Street Journal, Business Week, etc.).

There's not a thing wrong with working from your home, but make sure you have privacy and room for your equipment. You'll probably also need a copier and fax machine, postage meter and scale, and filing space. (All of this is legitimately deductible on tax returns, by the way.)

Also, find a lawyer and accountant who understand solo practice and small business, not your cousin Louie or the person who closed on your house. Incorporate immediately, as an LLC, a Chapter C, or a Subchapter S (your accountant can tell you which is best for your circumstances). Acquire errors and omissions (malpractice) insurance, liability insurance, and disability insurance. Find a web designer and start a Web site (or at least reserve the domain name).

Once again, those over 50 have some real advantages. We are far more credible as guest speakers. We've probably learned how to write decently to have articles published. We have the experience to make an interviewer interested in what we say. We belong to enough groups, past and present, to facilitate networking, and most likely have the requisite networking (also known as "schmoozing") skills.

And, most importantly, we probably have a slew of 50+ colleagues and acquaintances who have risen to positions that constitute potential buying points for us. Most importantly, it's far easier for a mature person to establish a peer-to-peer buyer relationship with a contemporary.

So, the real secret may be to ignore the purported drawbacks of age and focus on the very real advantages:

• A long-developed network of professional relationships
• An immediate peer rapport with buyers
• The experience to draw on examples and anecdotes
• The stature of an expert who has "been there and

done that"

• At least a minimum of financial and other support resources required for business investment

• Existing banking, legal, accounting and other key relationships

There is no time like the present for people over 50 to initiate and develop personal businesses, whether from need or from desire. Just remember, you face a marketing challenge, and people will not rush to your door. You must create the groundswell by building on the very history that has led you to where you are today.

21

Catch up on the films you missed

Give yourself credit; you're a classic. You deserve to be able to relax a little and take in some of the things you've missed.

BY SUSAN SEIDELMAN

Susan Seidelman graduated from NYU Film School with a Masters degree in the late 1970s. Her films include Desperately Seeking Susan, Making Mr. Right, and She Devil. Seidelman also has worked in television, has been nominated for Emmys as well as an Academy Award. She is currently editing her new feature The Boynton Beach Bereavement Club.

For me, turning 40 was more difficult than turning 50. I work in an industry that is very youth-oriented, so going from being a filmmaker in my 30s to one in my 40s, was the big leap. Once I was over that hurdle, turning 50 wasn't a big deal — I actually liked it. My son was born in my late 30s; prior to that, my time was spent with work. When I reached my 40s, I was all about family. By the time I turned

50, my son was becoming more self-sufficient, so now, I'm all about getting back to being me — and the endless challenge of figuring out how to combine work and family, and finally achieving comfort with who I am now.

I'm a film director, and I'm over 50. In my field, 50 is as much a gender issue as it is an age issue. The double whammy thing is going strong. In the film industry, people are always looking for the next new thing, whether that newest thing is the star or the director. But older directors like Martin Scorsese, Woody Allen, Francis Ford Coppola or Brian de Palma are considered masters. You don't really have that equivalent when it comes to women. Why? Probably because there aren't that many women past 50 who have been able to accumulate a significant body of work – maybe that's because the industry just hasn't afforded women the same kind of opportunities.

I started out directing films 23 years ago. "Desperately Seeking Susan" was my first studio movie. I remember in 1984 when I first walked onto that set, I was clearly one of the younger people, plus I was female, plus I was five feet tall. I probably looked like a P.A. (production assistant) – one of the crewmembers even asked me to get him a cup of coffee. Now, it's twenty years later, I just finished filming a movie in Florida, and when I walked onto that set I was referred to as "Mrs. Seidelman." I looked around. . . expecting to see my mother! I wasn't the oldest person in the crew, but I was now definitely one of the oldest.

What I really like about my age is that professionally, I have less to prove now. I know what I know, I know what I'm good at, and I also know what I don't know — and I'm not afraid to ask questions. For example, there is all this new digital technology, computer-generated effects, digital editing and other stuff that younger people take for granted. I'm not as familiar as some of the younger filmmakers with the new technology, but at this stage, I look at things differently: technology is just a tool. Along with age comes more life experience, and I think I have more insight into people and storytelling than I did when I was 30. I look at technology simply as a tool to tell interesting stories on film.

A big part of being a director is working with actors. I actually feel that getting older is an advantage; it has given me more experience working with people, I'm more patient, and I've learned how to get what I need in any given situation. And there's another factor — being a mother has also helped; I've become more maternal, patient, and tolerant, and I use those skills when I collaborate with actors . Years of experience (and learning from my mistakes) have enabled me to get what I need without getting someone's back up, or making them feel insecure or defensive.

As a director, the stories that most interest me have adult protagonists who are dealing with contemporary adult issues. Also, my films tend to be mostly character oriented and my interests sociological. I'm curious about how people deal with modern relationships — whether it's "Sex and The City" or "Desperately Seeking Susan". The movie I just finished filming in Florida is set in an "adult" gated community, and is about people in their 60s who suddenly find themselves single again and back in the "dating game" at this stage in their life — a time when they never expected to be dealing with that stuff again. I find it interesting that there are more and more "senior citizens", looking for love, companionship and sex. More seniors are dating and living together. And with all the new "sexual enhancement" drugs on the market, more seniors are having sex. The perception of getting older isn't what it used to be, now that the Baby Boomer generation is in its 50s and 60s. Think about it, Mick Jagger is a grandfather! The generation that were children in the 1950s, came of age in the 1960s, and are now in their 50s, will soon be approaching their 60s, and that will change the way we think about aging.

In terms of films, as you enter your 50s, I would definitely recommend catching up on some of the great ones that you may have missed. My personal list of favorites would be, "Citizen Kane," "Lawrence of Arabia," "Chinatown," "Brief Encounter," "Rebel without a Cause" and "North by Northwest." I'd also recommend some great American movies from the 1960s and 70s like "Raging Bull," "The Godfather," "Badlands," "Midnight Cowboy," "The Graduate," "The Last Picture Show" and "The Way We Were," as well as some Billy Wilder films, like "The Apartment" or "Some Like it Hot;" and some Woody Allen films like "Manhattan," "Broadway Danny Rose" and "Radio Days." I think everyone should see a Fellini film by the time they're 50 – my favorites are "Nights of Cabiria" and "Amacorde." Other foreign films I'd recommend are Francois Truffaut's "400 Blows," Hector Babenco's "Pixote," Lina Wertmuller's "Seven Beauties," John Boorman's "Hope and Glory," and Bernardo Bertolluci's "Last Tango In Paris" and "The Conformist."

Finally, I'd say the best thing about being 50 is that there is a kind of confidence that comes with age. Hopefully you've made peace with whatever direction your life has taken you, so there is no longer that pressure to have to prove anything to yourself or the world.

Section Six

MASTERING YOUR MONEY

22

Bulk up your portfolio's defense

Make sure your money keeps growing, even when the markets don't.

BY BILL GROSS

Gross is a founder and managing director of Pacific Investment Management Company (PIMCO), and oversees the $370 billion of fixed income securities. Gross, author of Everything You've Heard About Investing is Wrong (Times Books/Random House) is the only money manager to have been twice named Morningstar's Fixed Income Manager of the Year.

Home runs, slam-dunks, and go-for-broke downfield passes are the highlight moments in professional sports, but every coach will tell you it's defense that wins championships.

When it comes to investing, having a good defense means protecting your portfolio against potential pitfalls so that your money grows despite the inevitable market swings.

So, what are those pitfalls and how do you defend your portfolio against them?

I believe that one of the biggest long-term risks investors face is the potential for rising inflation...and at the end of the day, isn't one of the goals of investing to increase your ability to buy things in the future? Rising inflation means the dollars you invest today will buy less "things" in the future. Sure, inflation hasn't been much of a threat in recent decades, but as the saying goes, and the attorneys will like this line: "Past performance is no guarantee of future results."

What's happening is that there is an ongoing battle in the U.S. and global economies between the forces of inflation and the forces of deflation...and believe it or not, the biggest inflationary force today is the U.S. government. You see, the U.S. faces enormous debts, and the typical government response to huge debts is not to meet them but to inflate them away. The U.S. has been using its printing press to print mountains of dollars in an effort to do just that.

Deflationary forces, including cheap imports from China and the developed world's aging population, are strong as well. I don't know who will ultimately win, but in the past, the government and its printing press have been the victors...so I'd suggest bulking up your inflation defense. And you know what, turning 50 is a darn good milestone at which to take a another look at your portfolio to ensure that you are adequately protected against inflation.

A second significant long-term risk facing investors right now is the potential for a decline in the U.S. standard of living. The U.S. consumes too much and we pay for it with debt and a heavy dose of the rest of the world's savings, which they lend us so we can buy more of their stuff. Nevertheless, there will be a point where other nations will no longer be willing to subsidize our excesses... and it appears that we might be at the point right now.

Bottom line is that there is no easy fix for this imbalance in the global economy. For Americans to voluntarily begin to get "that old time religion" of saving more money is but a dream. And it seems equally unlikely that the government will be willing and/or able to move back to a balanced budget any time soon. As I noted earlier, the easiest solution, but not my preferred solution, is for the government to weaken the dollar and inflate the debt away.

The problem with this solution is that rising inflation, a declining dollar, and increasing overseas competition are all threats to the lifestyle that Americans enjoy today. As the dollar depreciates, the U.S. standard of living goes down. For example, as the value of the dollar falls, it's not just the trip to Europe you're planning that becomes more expensive, but all the imports that you buy become more expensive too. So, a 50-year-old (or anyone for that matter) has to defend against not only domestic inflation but also the risk of a declining standard of living in the U.S. compared to the rest of the world.

There are two steps you can take to defend your portfolio against these threats. First, invest in bonds that are protected against inflation, namely U.S. Treasury inflation-indexed securities, or "TIPS." TIPS can help defend your portfolio against inflation because these securities are protected one-for-one against a rise in consumer prices. When consumer prices rise, the U.S. Treasury adjusts the principle and interest on TIPS upward to counteract the inflationary effect. These securities should be a core holding for investors of all ages. Commodities and other physical assets, such as real estate, can also offer some protection against inflation, but the average 50-year old investor should carefully consider the higher risk that these investments can entail...the attorneys will like that caveat too.

The second step is to diversify your investments globally. Americans are just beginning to understand that a portion of their portfolio should be spread around to diversified markets as well as diversified currencies. Europeans understand this because, prior to the advent of the Euro, they had to trade and travel between countries using multiple currencies. They get it. Canadians understand this because they are one of America's largest trading partners...the continuing struggle between the Looney and the buck. They get it. Americans, except for that Spring-break trip to Cancun, don't really run into daily currency issues...so we're just on the brink of "getting it." Should the dollar continue to decline, American investors will come to understand the importance of global diversification – especially when they review their next quarterly statement. So, I'd recommend diversifying both currency-wise and market-wise.

So, when your offense goes flat, when the long bomb falls incomplete or the slam-dunk incredibly bounces off the rim, then a coach looks to his defense to hold the line.

Bulk up your defense by buying some inflation protection and diversifying globally...and if you do, the only thing you'll have to fret about... is turning 60...aggggh!!!

23

Rethink your insurance strategy

From life insurance to long-term care, the rules are different at midlife.

BY RICHARD BOWREN

Rich Bowren has spent 15 years helping clients meet their insurance planning needs. After graduating from West Chester University in 1987 with a BS degree in Economics, he went right to work for State Farm Insurance in 1988, and was appointed as a State Farm Agent in early 1990. He's a two-time President's Club Member, and a two-time Chairman's Circle Qualifier. In late 2004, Mr. Bowren was promoted into State Farm's Agency Field Leadership Program.

As we enter the later phase of our lives, we need to spend time evaluating our insurance needs. Insurance is serious business. There is an old joke in the industry about an agent working hard to sell a potential client a policy. "Don't let me frighten you into making a hasty decision, Mr. Fishbein," summed up the agent. "If you wake up tomorrow, call me."

But insurance is one of the necessary evils that we have to deal with in life. No one wants to run into a circumstance that requires insurance coverage, but occasionally life dishes up a batch of lemons, and insurance provides an opportunity to make lemonade.

When tackling insurance issues, the first thing to do is work with a professional to have a comprehensive review of all your insurance programs. Additionally, you should consider what other types of insurance may be needed in the future to protect you against exposure to risk, such as that incurred with travel and certain hobbies. Specifically, you need to examine your auto, homeowners, life, health, and disability insurance programs.

When doing a comprehensive review of your insurance programs, you should consider what type of lifestyle you hope to enjoy. Will you be traveling, staying at home occupied with hobbies, or working full-time or part-time? Will you want to start a business, pass a business to a family member, or sell the business? These and other considerations will impact your insurance decisions. Regardless of any decisions you make, it is extremely important that your spouse (if you are married) or your beneficiaries have a full understanding of all coverages, why they are in place, and who to contact in the event of a question or a claim.

You should evaluate your healthcare situation by asking questions like, do I have a traditional health plan, HMO, or PPO? Do I have the right to keep the plan if I change jobs? If so, what will be the cost? How long can I keep the coverage? As my medical needs change due to aging, will my policy pay for the services I may need? If I travel, what do

I need to do if emergency treatment is needed in the U.S. or abroad?

Health insurance is not only accident and sickness coverage, but is also Long Term Care (LTC) and disability insurance. Many people mistakenly think their health insurance or Social Security will pay all the costs associated with nursing homes, skilled nursing care, or custodial care. This is not the case. You should begin to seriously consider Long Term Care insurance as part of your insurance portfolio. The product is meant to protect your assets, and allow you to maintain your freedom of choice should you not be able to care for yourself due to an injury or illness.

And don't forget disability coverage when thinking about your insurance program. Again, be sure to look at your current income and benefits. Be sure your benefits are enough to cover your monthly expenses. If you have retired, and are still paying for disability coverage, will it pay the benefits promised? If the benefits are not sufficient, can you purchase more? There are limits on the amount of disability insurance an individual can purchase, so make sure you check with your agent.

Life insurance is an important subject to those who are turning 50, even though the majority of our earning years are behind us. Many risks and financial obligations are behind us. Mortgages may be lower or eliminated. Children's educations may be paid for, and savings plans may have had time to build up to the point of being able to generate income if needed. Whatever type of life insurance policies you own, be sure your beneficiaries are current and up-to-date. Unfortunately, this is very easily overlooked, but you want to be sure the benefit will be distributed according to your wishes.

If your employer is supplying any or all of your life insurance coverage, you should ensure that the coverage is convertible. If the coverage is not convertible to an individual policy, then you will lose that coverage when you leave the company. You might think that you will be able to replace your employer-supplied coverage, but keep in mind that you first must qualify and be insurable, which means you must be healthy. But be careful when you shop, as policies vary greatly from provider to provider.

Take another look at your auto insurance. Auto insurance is state regulated, and laws differ widely from state to state. If you have moved recently, or plan to move, you should have an in-depth conversation with a professional insurance agent, and be sure to ask for a full explanation of each type of coverage available. It isn't always wise to opt for the minimum medical coverage provided with your auto insurance policy. Make sure you ask what the price differences are, what is covered, what coverage is primary, and how your health insurance plays into an automobile accident situation. You might be able to save money on your comprehensive and collision coverage, which takes care of physical damage to your vehicle. As your assets have grown, you could probably reduce your premiums substantially by accepting more risk and taking a higher deductible.

The issues involved in evaluating your home insurance policy are not much different than with auto insurance. Do you have adequate liability insurance on your policy? Keep in mind that, while your homeowner's insurance policy covers your home and possessions, the policy is also the primary source of your personal liability protection, following you wherever you go. For example, if you are on a golf course and accidentally injure someone or damage property and are found liable for those damages, your homeowner's insurance should pay for your defense and indemnification costs. As for your home and its contents, check to make sure your policy covers your home's current replacement value. Ask your agent to re-value your home, and be sure your coverage is adequate. Does your policy cover your treasured items? Do you want them covered? What is the best way to replace them if they are destroyed or stolen? Do you have current documentation of what you own, including photos, receipts, and records?

As you have grown older, your assets have probably grown as well, thus creating the need for higher limits of liability protection. The cost of increasing liability limits is very small in comparison to the amount of coverage you can add to your present policy. It's important to make sure that your liability limits adequately protect your asset base, reducing your overall risk of exposure in case of accident or lawsuit. A major lawsuit could wipe out your entire savings, so you want to be certain to have adequate coverage. An excellent way to be sure you won't be financially ruined by a lawsuit is to purchase a liability umbrella policy. This policy is fairly inexpensive, and adds a significant amount of coverage to your auto and home liability coverage.

Once you've taken the time to assess your current levels of insurance coverage and the changing parameters of your assets and life situation, you'll have a clearer understanding of where you can cut back on insurance costs and where you need to supplement your program. It's important not to underestimate the importance of insurance as you plan for the future æ it can mean the difference between financial hardship and financial peace of mind.

24

Strengthen your will

No more excuses: Your family needs the protection that comes from a clear, up-to-date last will and testament.

BY REBECCA SMOLEN

Ms. Smolen is a Partner in WolfBlock's Private Client Services Practice Group. She concentrates her practice in the areas of tax and estate planning, closely held business succession planning, charitable giving, estate and trust administration, and tax-exempt organizations. Ms. Smolen has authored numerous articles and lectures frequently on various topics related to her practice areas.

While many people find estate planning complex, the idea behind it is simple: to control your assets during your lifetime while also leaving a legacy to those people and institutions you care about most. Having an estate plan in place is one of the most important steps you can take on behalf of your family and/or your business.

First, it is crucial that you select your Executor or Trustee for your estate. You need to find a person who you can trust with the administration of your estate and the administration of any trusts you create for your heirs. This could be an individual or a bank or trust company, but it must be someone who you feel comfortable will abide by your wishes.

It is also important to name people to handle your financial or health care affairs if you are unable. This means executing a General Power of Attorney, Health Care Power of Attorney and Living Will. For a Living Will, it is important to determine how you feel about the administration of life sustaining medical treatment (including nutrition and hydration) in the event you are terminally ill, permanently unconscious or suffering from another impaired health condition where the benefits of life may be outweighed by its burdens.

If you have children under 18, be sure you have identified guardians in the event you and the other parent die before they reach legal adult age (18 in most states). Also, consider what resources and assets will be available to your children and spouse should you die before your children become adults. You should reevaluate your need for life insurance and disability coverage depending on what you feel your family's needs might be if you are no longer able to provide for them. You may also want to consider Long Term Care insurance to alleviate the burden on your family should you require any kind of hospitalization or long term care in a facility.

Next, calculate your net worth (assets plus life insurance death benefits, less liabilities). Make sure you consider potential future inheritances from parents and/or others when estimating this figure. If your total net worth exceeds

$1,000,000, be sure to consult with an estate planning attorney who is an expert in Federal estate tax planning (under Federal estate tax laws, the Federal estate tax may come into play if you die with more than $1,000,000, in which case Federal estate tax rates can be as high as 55%). In this situation your estate planning documents should be structured to minimize the estate tax hit, and you may want to consider a structured gifting program to reduce the amount of your estate that will ultimately be subject to taxation.

Regardless of your net worth amount, you must evaluate what portions of your estate you wish to be divided between your spouse, children, charities, and others. Additionally, you need to decide whether money for individuals (i.e. spouse, children or others) should be given outright or in trust, keeping in mind various protection issues for your heirs and "affluenza" issues (i.e. when children inherit enough money so they don't have to work and may get themselves in trouble with "idle hands").

If your parents are living, talk to them about whether they've addressed the above issues, and if not, make a priority of helping them get their affairs in order. If they have, get a sense of how they have set up their affairs, and evaluate whether your financial situation should impact how they plan their estates. For example, if you are very well off, it may make sense for them to set aside your "share" of their assets for your children, being mindful of Federal generation skipping tax issues. If you have creditor issues (i.e., if you are a doctor who is concerned about medical malpractice claims), it may be wise to suggest they put your inheritance in trust so it is inaccessible to creditors.

The issues surrounding inheritance are particularly important to the Baby Boomer generation. Baby Boomers are stepping into the largest inheritance ever, some $10.4 trillion in total. On average, they're expected to receive around $90,000 each, with the top 10% of inheritors taking in a cool half-million each. But unfortunately, experts say, boomers are largely unprepared. In many cases, parents – who've put a lot of effort into setting aside a bequest – haven't given the actual transfer of wealth a great deal of thought either.

That can be a costly mistake. Inheritances can be frittered away by mismanagement, lost to estate taxes or drained by court battles. So how do you make the most of an inheritance? Here are a few tips:

*Do nothing. Not forever, of course, but for the first six months to a year, stash any money you receive in a safe haven – such as a money-market or certificate-of-deposit account – and do little else. Keep going to work. Keep your spending in check. Why? There's a temptation to splurge to avoid the reality that you've lost a loved one. If you're able to first go through the grieving process, you have a much better chance of making good financial decisions later.

*Look at your debts first. Before investing or spending any money you receive, consider whether it makes more sense to use it to pay down existing credit card or other debt. If your credit card is racking up interest at 18 percent, for example, and you think you'd earn only 8-10% by investing the money, you are better off paying off your cards. But if you have a bottom-of-the-barrel interest rate on your credit card, say 7%, or if you'll use the bequest to pay down your 7% mortgage, you may do better by investing.

*Hire help. For bequests of $20,000 or more, it's wise to have a financial adviser to make sure you make the best use of it. If you receive more than $250,000, you need an entire team: a lawyer, a financial planner, a broker, an insurance agent and an accountant. Conduct interviews to find the right people. Ask for a 15- to 20-minute informational appointment and then ask each person what he or she would do in your situation. One question to ask yourself is: Do I feel comfortable, or intimidated? You may be tempted to use your parents' advisers, but you need people who will treat you like an adult, not brush aside your questions because they still think of you as an 8-year-old.

Whatever you do, don't wait to take control of your estate planning. You'll find that you will look to the future with greater security and confidence, and your family will thank you for your efforts. ☼

25

Budget to your 100th birthday

The odds of you making it another 50 years are better than ever. Here's what you need to know to make sure you can live well, not just long.

by Eric Friedman

Eric Friedman is a Retirement Consulting Actuary for Watson Wyatt Worldwide. He is a Fellow of the Society of Actuaries, an Enrolled Actuary, and a Member of the American Academy of Actuaries.

The lifestyles of people over 50 have changed dramatically over the last 100 years. Before 1900, retirement was virtually unheard of. Most people worked their entire adult lives, and the few who did retire did not need the extensive financial preparations necessary today, due to shorter life expectancies.

But these days, with increased longevity and retirement more common, financial planning has become challenging. Although life expectancy has increased only modestly relative to total lifespan, it is a huge increase when viewed as a percentage of life expectancy beyond the average retirement age. In 1940, the average life expectancy of a 65-year-old was 12.7 years for males and 14.7 for females. By 2040, those figures are projected to be 18.6 and 21.7 years respectively, representing a 50% increase in life expectancy . Since about half the population will outlive the average life expectancy, people should plan on saving enough to support themselves many years beyond their average life expectancy.

The trend of opting for earlier retirement compounds the challenge. As modern medicine improves the health and quality of life of elderly people, it would be possible to delay retirement — but this hasn't been the case. In fact, people are retiring earlier than they used to. In 1950, 46% of men over age 65 were in the workforce; by the mid-1990s, that figure fell to only 16% . Put simply, tomorrow's retirees will need to save much more than yesterday's retirees. In addition, in the past, children commonly became self-sufficient by the late teens, however many parents now support their children through college and graduate school. This continuing financial burden erodes the ability of some 50-year-olds to save for retirement.

The traditional model for retirement income is the "three-legged stool": Social Security, employer-sponsored pension plans, and personal savings (the amount you put into your retirement savings, usually through stock, bond, and mutual fund investments, and investments in tax-deferred vehicles like 401(k) plans and IRAs). By combining the "replacement ratio" — the proportion of post-retirement income to pre-retirement earnings — and the three-legged stool, we can form a simple model for retirement income needs. To maintain pre-retirement lifestyle, a common rule of thumb is that income from all three legs of the stool should total at least 70-80% of pre-retirement income. (The target replacement ratio is usually less than 100% because retirees have lower expenses: lower taxes, no need to save for retirement, no work-related expenses such as commuting costs, etc.)

1. Social Security. This program was never designed to be the sole source of retirement income for most people, though some retirees have used it that way. Social Security was intended to be a financial safety net, providing benefits closer to minimum subsistence levels. Although legislative changes to Social Security are debated, the expected benefit amount upon retirement probably will not change much. Go to the Social Security Administration's Web site at http://www.ssa.gov to calculate your estimated benefits.

2. Employer-sponsored pension plans. The benefit levels of pension plans vary, but government employees and those who have stayed in their jobs generally receive better benefits. Recently, many employers have overhauled their pension plans; make sure you understand your benefits from every previous employer, and contact them if you're not sure what you're entitled to.

3. Personal savings. This is the area where you have the most control, but there is no simple formula to determine how much you should save. The primary rule is simply that the assets should be sufficient to generate the remainder of

the income you need for retirement. A person with an average or below-average employer-sponsored pension plan will need more personal savings than someone with more generous employer-provided benefits.

All three legs of the stool should be considered during financial planning; otherwise the stool will become wobbly. One challenge is that some benefits are stated as annuity amounts, payable for life (e.g., $1,000 monthly pension); and others as single sum account balances (e.g., $100,000 in a 401(k) account.) It can be difficult to project total future savings, since one is stated as a lump sum and the other as periodic income. Compounding the problem is that investment returns can fluctuate significantly, and you must also make necessary adjustments for inflation, taxes, and your uncertain life expectancy.

A rough rule of thumb for equating a single lump sum to annual inflation-indexed annuity payments is to divide the single sum amount by a factor of 14 (corresponding to a 20-year retirement, assuming 7% investment returns and 3% inflation) to 22 (corresponding to a 35-year retirement, assuming 6% investment returns and 3% inflation). Because none of us knows exactly how long we will live or what our investment returns will be, it is necessary to evaluate our risk tolerances, make conservative guesses, and plan accordingly. For example, if we use a median number of 18, a single sum of $180,000 at retirement equates to receiving $10,000 annually, increased for inflation. It is fairly common to need several hundred thousand dollars in personal savings to retire without reducing your standard of living, and optimism is a poor substitute for conservative financial planning. Consider using a financial planner or financial planning books and tools that will provide sophisticated analysis tailored to your individual needs.

As times change, the concept of retirement is also evolving. The traditional three-legged-stool has been growing a fourth leg: income from part-time work after a person retires from his or her primary job. Research on phased retirement done by Watson Wyatt Worldwide shows an increasing number of people are transitioning into retirement gradually, slowly reducing the hours they work, instead of exiting the workforce abruptly.

Broad demographic trends are also likely to have a significant, and possibly negative, impact on society. Three major trends—decreasing fertility rates, increasing life expectancy, and the retirement of the Baby Boomer generation—will dramatically boost the number of retirees per worker. In the United States, the Social Security Administration estimated that the number of beneficiaries per 100 workers is expected to increase from 30 in 2003 to 46 in 2030 —an increase of more than 50%. Most nations in the developed world are facing similar situations .

Some speculate that these demographic trends foreshadow too few workers in the developed world to produce the goods society demands. Others hypothesize that as the proportion of people saving assets for retirement declines, and the proportion of people selling assets to fund their retirement increases, prices of stocks and bonds may plummet . The combination of worker shortages and declining asset markets could force later retirement ages for the typical worker because they will need to work longer to fund their retirement. Globalization and economic productivity increases will be able to make up part of the shortfall, but if they fail to increase sufficiently, the overall standard of living will likely decline.

There's an old Spanish proverb that says "He who does not look ahead remains behind." Fortunately, actuarial tools allow us to look into the future more clearly and more productively. And that should result in a more secure financial future for every 50-something. ☀

26

Get smart about the IRS

Paying taxes is inevitable, but it can hurt less than you think.

BY BRAD HALL

As the Managing Director of his own firm, Hall & Company, Brad Hall is actively involved in all aspects of taxation, auditing, and business planning. He has over twenty-six years of experience in public accounting. In addition, Brad spends a great deal of time consulting in the area of business management, business succession planning, estate planning and preparation of comprehensive personal financial plans.

You have to admire the Internal Revenue Service. Any organization that makes that much money without advertising deserves our respect. And respect it we must, especially when we turn the magic age of 50 and have to lay out a financial plan for the rest of our lives. Tax planning is a critical part of such a plan, encompassing a wide array of financial planning issues. Fortunately, there is a clear path to tax planning.

Planning to properly insure against any risk to retirement will protect your ability to retire in style. Many people fail to insure the risks until it is too late. For instance, life insurance should be taken out when you are still healthy, hopefully by age 50. The same applies to Long Term Care insurance.

From purely a tax standpoint, the IRS allows specific tax breaks for you once you reach 50 æ you are entitled to higher deductible retirement options called "catch-up contributions." You become eligible to contribute an additional $500 each year into your IRA each year, in addition to the regular $3,000 contribution. If you participate in your company's SIMPLE IRA, you are able to contribute an additional $2,000 each year into the plan, in addition to the maximum $10,000. Individuals who will attain age 50 before the end of the tax year are generally permitted to make additional deferrals. There are similar eligible "catch-up" stipulations in SIMPLE IRAs or SIMPLE 401(k) plans that also may allow additional deferrals. If you are self-employed, you might consider a SEP (Simplified Employee Pension).

Long Term Care insurance can protect your assets if you are disabled by a chronic physical or mental illness. The Health Insurance Portability and Accountability Act of 1996 (HIPAA) was designed to encourage consumers to purchase Long Term Care (LTC) insurance through tax deduction incentives for premiums, and exclusions from income for benefits received. These incentives were offered to decrease the growing burden of long-term healthcare placed on Medicare and Medicaid.

Medicare will pay for up to 100 days of care in a qualified skilled nursing facility, following a hospital stay of at least three consecutive days. However, Medicare is designed for skilled medical and nursing care of acute illnesses, not long-term custodial care for chronic disabling physical or mental illnesses.

Medicaid pays for long-term care, but only if the person in need of care is impoverished æ in most cases, single patients can have no more than $2,000 in nonexempt resources. In addition, the individual must contribute a sizable portion of his or her income towards the cost of care. Careful planning and asset transfers may allow an individual to qualify. However, in most cases, people are not willing to transfer assets to their children and lose control over their long-term care.

The National Association of Insurance Commissioners (NAIC) in "A Shopper's Guide to Long-Term Care Insurance" warns that an individual should not consider purchasing LTC insurance if he or she cannot afford the premiums, has limited assets, receives only Social Security benefits or Supplemental Security Income (SSI) as income, and has trouble paying for utilities, food, medicine, or other important needs. The NAIC recommends that an individual consider purchasing LTC insurance if he or she has significant assets and income to protect, can afford to pay for his or her own care, and wishes to stay independent of the support of others.

You should also consider reviewing your home mortgage debt at age 50. If you have a 30-year mortgage that you will be paying until age 80, yet would like to retire at age 65, you should consider either refinancing with a 15-year fully amortized loan, or determine the amount needed to fully fund your existing mortgage on a monthly basis to be mortgage debt free by age 65.

Certain Social Security benefits are available upon reaching age 50. A surviving spouse is entitled to survivor's benefits if the deceased worker was fully insured and the surviving spouse is at least age 65; or, age 50, disabled, and married to the worker for at least nine months prior to the worker's death; or, is the parent of the worker's natural or adopted child.

In this day and age, turning 50 is no big deal. As they say in all the self-help books, 50 is the new 30. And once you reach that milestone, you still have a long way to go æ and a lot to prepare for. That's especially true when it comes to your taxes and your financial affairs. So don't wait until it's too late. Get going today and ensure financial comfort in your Golden Years.

27

Embrace your inner Trump

Why 50 is the perfect time to invest in real estate.

BY JOANNE ATWELL

Jo-Anne E. P. Atwell has an education in Business Management, Marketing, Sales, and Airline and Travel. Before earning her real estate license, Joanne was business development director for NovaCare Rehabilitation in Philadephia. She is currently working for Prudential Fox & Roach in Doylestown and is a member of Pennsylvania Association of Realtors as well as Bucks County Board of Realtors.

R eal estate is all about opportunity. When you see an opening, don't wait. There is an old saying that "opportunity is a bird that never perches for too long." The good news in my line of business is that real estate can be a great opportunity for investing. It's especially suited to those hitting the 50-year mark.

Why? At this stage in life, you probably have enough assets or equity saved up to be able to consider the purchase of real estate as a serious addition to your investment portfolio. And unlike your younger counterparts who do not have the asset base to invest in real estate, or seniors who cannot afford to invest the time it takes to make a real estate purchase pay off over time, you are at the perfect point in life to capitalize on this valuable market.

Let's look first at the investment property market. According to recent statistics published by the U.S. Census Bureau, 75% of multi-family investors are over the age of 45. Over half of these (51.6%) own less than five units, and they earned approximately 31% of their income from ownership of rental properties. These statistics may surprise you, but some logical reasons explain these numbers. Most real estate investors come to the market later in life because they are concerned about their retirement, are at their highest potential earning power, or have inherited money or real estate.

There are four major reasons that an investor might choose real estate for investment:

1. Cash flow: With the right choice of property, it is possible to have a cash flow return after all other expenses have been covered, including mortgage, vacancy factor, repairs, property management, etc. Most banks will not lend money to buy a property if there is no hope of a cash flow return.

2. Appreciation: Loosely applying the rules of supply and demand, we can rest assured that with our current immigration patterns and population growth, there will be a continued need for housing over the next 50 years. You can safely assume a 4% appreciation level. Of course, some years will better than others, depending upon supply and demand and the increased costs of construction and

land/infrastructures.

The average single family home sold for $23,400 in 1970; in 2000, a similar average home sold for $169,000. That is an approximate 8% annual increase. Of course, appreciation will vary with the location and condition of the property, as well as the condition of the local economy.

3. Equity build-up: You reduce your mortgage and increase your equity with every mortgage payment made on underlying debt. A portion of your payment goes toward reducing the principal. The shorter the loan period, the faster the equity builds.

4. Tax savings: Uncle Sam allows everyone but real estate brokers to depreciate their investment properties on Schedule E when filing annual tax returns. Residential properties depreciate over 27.5 years and commercial properties depreciate over 39 years.

You may be ready to jump at all of these opportunities to make money. Bear in mind, though, that the government needs to pay its bills and they get their share when you sell one of your investments. When you sell a property, you will be faced with a capital gains tax on the increase in value of the property. This cost could be deferred if you complete a 1031 tax deferred exchange to trade up from property to property, but ultimately the tax will come due.

Think through the following example: With $500,000 you can buy a $1,500,000 investment that may give you an 8% cash flow, an annual 4% appreciation, an annual equity build and a depreciation of $43,000 a year. This comes in at over a 20% annual return and should make you feel like you have made the right investment decision.

Regardless of the size of your real estate investment, you can make a return and build up your retirement. It is important to not buy the first investment that comes along; rather you should purchase the best investment. Pick an investment that you are the most comfortable with, maybe your grandmother's duplex. This will give you a chance to make some small mistakes and plan a long-term future investing in real estate. Choose a real estate agent who has some of his or her own investments to help you, and a property management company with good references.

Another way to take advantage of real estate returns is simply by purchasing a second home in an attractive area. The U.S. second home market is gearing up for what is virtually certain to be a series of record years for sales volume. And new research suggests that many more buyers are jumping into that market to make money, not to spend weekends at the beach sipping margaritas.

Whereas just 20% of second home buyers in the beginning of the 21st century were motivated primarily by investment returns, nearly double that (37%) now rank rental income as their primary objective. The study defined "investment" properties as those rented out for an aggregate six or more months per year, and rarely if ever used personally by the owners. Traditional "non-investment" second homes, by contrast, are primarily purchased for personal use and only sporadically rented out.

Why the dramatic switch? The "slumping stock market" and the continuing high appreciation and capital gains from residential real estate have grabbed the attention of the Baby Boomers. While the stock market has seen significant volatility in recent years, residential property has been gaining value impressively. Nationwide, home values are up by an average 38% since the turn of the century, according to the Office of Federal Housing Enterprise Oversight. But for many resort areas on the East and West coasts and in resort communities elsewhere, average gains have been even higher. Some well-located properties along the mid-Atlantic coast have doubled in resale value since 1997.

Just who are these new, investment-minded Baby Boomers snapping up resort condos and homes? The typical purchaser is 56-years-old, married, with no children under age 18 or living at home, and is relatively affluent, with an average household income of $92,000. And nearly 30% of all buyers expect to convert their second homes into their primary homes sometime in the future.

For example, a married couple in their mid-50s right now could buy a second home in a resort community, rent it out for the next five to seven years, then sell their principal home tax-free, and convert the rental home to their new principal residence. That would start the tax clock ticking again on their resort residence, and allow them to pocket all gains on the house tax-free (up to the $500,000 limit) after just 24 months of ownership and use.

So, if you're 50 or over, it's worth considering real estate very carefully when thinking about your long-term financial and residential goals. The payoff could be much greater than you ever imagined.

28

Give something back

**You know how to earn it; you know how to spend it.
But do you know how to give it away?**

BY LORNA WENDT

Lorna Wendt is the founder of Equality in Marriage Institute,
as well as the founding benefactor and board member of the
Women's Philanthropy Institute. She serves on the advisory
boards of Outward Bound USA, and the University of
Wisconsin's School of Music and College of Letters and
Sciences. In 2001, Worth Magazine named Wendt one of the
ten most influential people in the way Americans view money.

I have found the fifth decade of my life to be a rewarding
time of great self-discovery. I have been able to take all
the experiences and resources garnered during my life
and use them to accomplish my dreams and make my personal agenda for change a reality.

After more than thirty years of marriage to the CEO of
General Electric Capital, during which I worked to support
my husband's education, maintained our household, and

raised our children, I was facing divorce and a small settlement offer of 10% of our household assets. While the offer was a significant amount of money, I felt that accepting it would compromise my principles and disregard my role as an equal partner in our marriage. I decided to fight back and I filed for divorce first. I put together a stellar team of legal and financial advisors. And I called The Wall Street Journal. A year before my divorce, my fairly predictable existence as a household manager and corporate supporter would not have allowed me to imagine the things that would follow. Our divorce truly became the "split heard 'round the world." From the cover of Fortune to 20/20 to Oprah, I found myself defending the whole concept of equality in marriage.

In the end, I was awarded 50% of our hard assets and had started a national dialogue on the value of stay-at-home spouses and the concept of equal partnerships. There I was, a 54-year-old woman on the other side of a precedent -setting divorce, wondering, "What do I do now?" As tempting as it might have been to step out of the spotlight, I felt I was on the cusp of fully discovering my potential and using my experiences to make a difference.

Philanthropy has always been an important part of my life. As the daughter of a minister, I was raised to be benevolent, help others, and try and make the world a better place. Charity is also a very important part of being the wife of a corporate leader and, throughout my marriage, I was involved in many different causes. After my divorce, I made it my mission to use my resources to make a difference and create change in the areas that were most important to me. And I learned very quickly the difference between simply being philanthropic and truly finding and establishing your voice by helping others and making steps toward accomplishing your goals.

What I did was to take the lessons I learned and some of the money, and I founded The Equality in Marriage Institute. This philanthropic endeavor is a non-profit organization that encourages men and women to actively manage their partnerships to make them stronger, healthier, and more balanced. It also provides information, resources, and support to help people build, maintain and, if necessary, dissolve their partnerships and marriages. It also helps people facing divorce educate themselves so they can handle the emotional and financial transitions.

Education and helping people obtain the skills they need to manage and empower their lives has become a primary focus of my philanthropic voice.

Instead of donating small amounts of money and time to a long list of diverse causes, I found it more satisfying and life affirming to focus more of my time and resources toward the causes most important to me. And in embracing philanthropy, not just by writing checks, but also by creating my own personal agenda, I learned that I could use my voice and resources to make a difference in the world. This can work for anyone.

The following tips can help each of you use your life's

journey to create your own philanthropic voice and empower yourself by helping others and improving the world around you.

Think About It

No matter your occupation or life's experiences, we have all been involved with issues or situations that made us form opinions or want to do something to create change. Regardless of what the media or those around you say is most critical and urgent, think of what is most important to you, what most inspires you, and what motivates you to get involved.

Educate Yourself

Once you have pinpointed some philanthropic areas that motivate you to action, spend some time researching them. What is currently being done? What needs to be done? What organizations are on the forefront and what are the different ways you could get involved?

Be Innovative

There are many organizations and community groups doing invaluable philanthropic work in many areas that need your support. However, sometimes there may not be an existing entity that is addressing the problems you think are important. In my case, there wasn't a non-profit organization focused on the issues surrounding marriage and divorce that I found important, so I started my own. Look carefully for organizations that align with your vision, but don't be afraid to be innovative and create something new.

Get Involved

Money is an important component of most philanthropic efforts, but it is much more rewarding to give more than just cash. Supplement financial donations with the gift of your time, ideas, or contacts. Getting involved helps keep you educated and increases that feeling of progress and knowledge that you are really making a difference.

Be Humble, But Loud

No one wants to be that person accused of being charitable just to get attention. The reward of philanthropy isn't recognition, it is the empowerment of using your voice and your resources to create change. While it is noble to be humble, it is also important to share your philanthropic experiences with your friends and your community to encourage them to identify their passions and get involved in the causes important to them.

It doesn't matter how much money you have to contribute. It doesn't matter whether you have a great deal of time to volunteer or just a few hours a month. It doesn't matter if you are 35, 54, or 68. It's never too late to create a vision for helping others and promoting positive changes. Take time to look at the world around you and choose the specific areas where you want to make a difference; it's such an empowering and fulfilling endeavor. Focusing your voice and your resources on the things that are most important to you lets you feel first-hand the power of your actions and thrive in a sense of accomplishment and purpose.

Section Seven

HAVING FUN
LIKE A GROWN-UP

29

Get your mojo working

The only thing better than having more sex is having more good sex. Yes, it *does* get better with age.

BY MARC C. GITTELMAN, M.D.

Marc Gittelman, M.D. completed his surgical and urology training in New York City at the Mount Sinai Medical Center, where he received numerous awards. He founded and directs the Miami Center for Sexual Health. Dr. Gittelman has contributed to many journal publications, reviews and essays in the field of sexual health. He also writes a regular column on sexual health for the Miami Herald.

A re you worried that your sex life might be going in the same direction as your face and thighs? If so, don't fret. I'm here to tell you that sex is like a fine wine — it should only improve with age. That's because sexual satisfaction is so closely linked to emotional and partner satisfaction. And we know from the medical literature that satisfaction within a relationship tends to increase over time.

So how can you continue to make your sex life as thrilling as you remember it from your 20s? Or, if you are one of the lucky couples who still have "steamy" romantic interludes, maybe you're asking: how can I make sure the hot sexual temperature of my relationship doesn't fade?

The answer is the same: we need to understand and overcome some of the obstacles we encounter as we age, including the physical and hormonal changes our bodies inevitably undergo. Just as important, you need to face the challenge of keeping the intimacy and passion in your relationship new and fresh, regardless of how many years you've been together.

I'm going to start with the male side of the equation. But don't worry, ladies. Your turn is coming.

With the arrival of Viagra on the sexuality scene in 1999, phrases like "erectile dysfunction" suddenly became as common as sunflowers in August. Viagra', and the two drugs that followed, Cialis' and Levitra', addressed a fairly simple concept: as men age, the blood supply to all their organs — including the sexual organs — decreases.

Throw medical problems like diabetes, high blood pressure, obesity, and the use of certain medications into the mix, and it's no wonder that by age 50, nine out of 10 men have had at least one of "those" times (you know, the kind in which you're assured that this "happens to every man at one time or another.")

Be glad you live in the post-Viagra age. Today, more than 30 million men have used at least one of the three available drugs that, studies find, can resolve erection problems in over 80% of men. Knowing that having and maintaining an erection won't be a problem brings a renewal of shared intimacy and lovemaking — and a stronger relationship.

Bottom line: Don't be afraid to talk to your doctor about a once-verboten subject: your sex life.

Then it's time to figure out how to get your partner as interested as you are.

A well-respected study on sexuality from the University of Chicago found that 67% of women say they think about sex from a few times a week to a few times a month. Compare that to the men surveyed, 54% of whom said they think about sex at least once a day, often several times a day. It gives new meaning to the phrase "sexual differences."

However, what's even more interesting is that the same survey found that while men are mostly interested in sex, women want romance and love. Nearly eight out of 10 women surveyed said they enjoyed the caressing and hugging before intercourse far more than sex itself. And men? Well, nearly the same percentage said they viewed foreplay as nothing more than a necessary prelude to sex.

Take this dichotomy and add in declining hormone levels, physical changes, and the dual or triple roles most middle-aged women play today and it's no wonder researchers find that nearly 35% of women say they have a low sex drive. Additionally, one-fourth say they have difficulty achieving satisfactory orgasm, one-fourth note a decrease in their sexual arousal (both physical and psychological), and nearly 15% say they have some physical pain during sex.

Today, there is a new specialty devoted to treating female sexual dysfunction. It uses a team approach to evaluate and treat women who have problems with desire, arousal, or orgasm and who feel these challenges create difficulties for them or their partners.

Unfortunately, the medical treatment side of things for women lags far behind that for men. However, a multitude of potential treatments are in the research pipeline, including a testosterone patch that may help replace low levels of a woman's testosterone (which plays a major role in her sex drive, just as it does in a man's)...so stay tuned.

All the pills in the world won't improve your sex life, however, if your mind isn't into it. So the first step in revitalizing your sex life should be a commitment to improve the intimacy of your relationship.

Here is my own three-step plan:

1. Revive the emotional components of your relationship. Start doing fun and interesting things together like taking romantic vacations, planning surprise dinners of caviar and champagne, signing up for tango lessons. While spontaneity is great, the most effective way to integrate romance into your life is to have a planned "date." Planned sex can, and should be, a part of these dates.

2. Be a better "soul mate."

For the men, this means:

Listening to her and making those moments of communication count. That means turning the television off, putting the newspaper down, and looking at her while she's talking.

Appreciating her work demands/home demands/child demands and making an effort to be part of her team, not just a "helper."

Telling her how much you really love her and then showing her with nonverbal cues such as hand holding, sensual and non-sensual touching, and gift giving.

For the ladies this means:

Learning how to "play" with your partner. Consider taking an active part in or at least pretending to be interested in sports or other activities he would love to share with you.

Packing away the cotton briefs and pulling out the silky lingerie.

Entertaining his fun sexual fantasies (and making sure he entertains yours).

Telling him that he is the "greatest" lover. Eventually, he will be.

3. Enhance your own sensuality and sexuality. You need to reawaken your senses to see, feel, listen to, and touch the person in front of you as though you were seeing, feeling and touching him or her for the very first time. Part of this is mindset, and there are several games or exercises that work very, very well.

Pretend this is your first date. Look at one another as if this were the first time you were seeing and smelling each other. Flirt. And when it feels right, make the kiss as special and slow and romantic as that very first kiss was.

Show your partner the areas of your body that you want touched. I teach lovers to use red and green sticky dots, putting the green (for "go") dots on hot and ready spots, and the red (for "stop") dots on the prohibited or cautious zones. Maybe even a few yellow ones for "go slow." This game provides a wonderful opportunity for sexual communication and exploration and you and your lover are sure to have a few fun surprises along the way.

When all is said and done, sexuality is about achieving a meld of body, mind and soul with your lover. In your 20s, this was often driven by your body's response to raging hormones. By the time you reach 50, you've reached a time for reawakening and appreciating what you have around you, a time of rediscovering your lover and all that is amazing about him or her.

With this maturity, your body can enjoy sexual intimacy at a level of total and complete satisfaction that would have been impossible to achieve when you were younger.

30

Drive a race car

Admit it: You're dying to try something dirty, noisy, expensive, frightening, exhilarating, terrifying, and downright dangerous. What are you waiting for? You ain't getting any younger!

BY ED MCCABE

An adventurer and author as well as a successful advertising man, Ed McCabe was the first American to drive the grueling Paris/Dakar Rally. His book about that experience, Against Gravity, was published by Warner Books. He has written on both business and adventure in The New York Times, Playboy, Esquire, The Automobile, New York Magazine and other publications.

Few things you can do in life are as dirty, noisy, uncomfortable, expensive, exhausting, frightening, exhilarating, terrifying, and downright dangerous as driving a race car. In fact, can you think of any other endeavor that can even lay claim to as many diverse adjectives? What other pastime offers up so many obvious and persuasive reasons for not doing it? But strapping yourself into a 300-horsepower racing machine and popping the clutch might be the best way to break through the age 50 barrier.

Having done it, I can tell you this: nothing you will ever attempt (nothing legal anyhow) will give you the same rapturous feeling of having gotten away with something.

But that's just the slightly twisted and quirky explanation for what motivates a human to travel so fast on land that the field of vision becomes narrowed by half while color perception evaporates into a dreamlike state, where only the gray shred of a colorless thread separates life from possible death.?

Note to women: race car driving tends to be a man's sport, though I know more female racing drivers than female football players. The motivation for women to drive race cars will likely be at least a little different from that of men, who indeed most likely exhibited this inclination at the age of three when pushing a ketchup bottle across the kitchen floor, going "vroom-vroom!"

The fact is, people of different sexes, ages, and sizes drive racing cars. Anyone with some innate craziness, however infinitesimal, and the desire, determination, and money to do it, can do it. The latter is the only requirement that keeps the sport from being wholly democratic.

Once you had to drive fast in unacceptable and unexpected places to practice this calling. Buy a car, show up somewhere at a race. Didn't matter what kind. Win. Then it's got you like nothing will ever get you.

Part of you loves it, part of you hates it, but inescapably now, all of you, in every pore and breath and circumstance, needs it. Until you've tasted victory, you'll never understand the disgusting smell of defeat. You need that element of competitiveness in you.

I know a 40-ish mother of three who started racing because it was something she could share with her husband that wasn't golf. Now, she loves it because it helps her forget her husband and her family. She says that she also likes being better than the person in the next car.

Another racing friend likes racing because of the feeling it gives him in his ass. Like it's physically on the line and he can feel completely the margin of danger and safety he's traveling on. That's maybe the ultimate feeling of control. But he also likes learning. Knows that that's what racing is: the search for a faster line through a turn, the ever deeper dives into corners before braking, the squirrelly feeling of the card edging around disaster. That ass feel.

He likes the camaraderie. The sharing of a uniquely individual experience others share generically, lost as they are in their own individuality. That's a club.

If you haven't done it before, you can try it without commitment; just try to be as good as you can be in that moment. There are racing driver's schools all over the U.S., in Canada, Europe and Australia. You can find one just about anywhere you're likely to find yourself.

But if you think you have the itch you'd better scratch it soon. Fifty is about the age most people start thinking of preserving what's left of their existence rather than squandering it. Sure, Paul Newman is still driving competitively at eighty. But he started young, at forty.

There are schools for learning to competitively drive

almost any kind of car you ever dreamed of driving. From 4-wheel drives, to go-karts, to sleek sports-racing cars to open-wheel formula cars to NASCAR-type stock cars. Name your poison. Sign up. Learn. Even if you don't have the craziness to go on to compete and win, you'll gain a lot from the experience.

Give yourself a day on the wet skid pad pulling G's, controlling a near-uncontrollable car with the throttle alone. Get out on the track and put your foot to the floor and your heart into your mouth.

You'll learn the true meaning of getting your priorities straight. There's no time for thinking, only for doing right and not doing wrong. All else is superfluous.

Great training for the rest of your life.

31

Play golf in Scotland

**Nothing will spark — or even rekindle — your love
for the game like a trip to the land where golf began.**

BY BILL DANIELS

Bill Daniels is the founder and CEO of the Golf Chicago
Group, a multi-media communications, publishing and consulting company. He first went to Scotland in 1992. He also is
on the Board of the First Tee of North Chicago, and in July
of 2004 played 90 holes of golf in one day, walking and carry-
ing his bag while raising nearly $10,000 in pledged donations
for the First Tee.

The decade of your 50s — whether you're 50, 55, or 58
— is the perfect time for you to rekindle the passion for
golf you might have had at an earlier age. And if that
passion has not died out, if it is still burning with a white
heat, what I am about to suggest to you post-50 golfers will
only deepen your commitment to this marvelous lifelong
game. In fact, do these three things and I guarantee that the
game of golf will sustain and satisfy you for the next two or
three decades — easily!

First, pay a visit to legendary Scotland, golf's historical birthplace. It was there that golf began, and anyone who considers themselves a complete golfer should seize the opportunity to play the country's windswept links and the highland's hidden gems (as for those of you who are shaking your heads saying, "been there, done that" — just hang on. I've got something for you, too).

Golf in Scotland is more than just a game; it is part of the Scottish way of life, as integral to its society as firecrackers are to our Fourth of July. Indeed, the Scots seem born with some special insight or secret vision when it comes to golf. They instinctively appreciate the deepest mysteries that the game holds, not to mention the insistent grip it can have on the soul. If you let it, golf in Scotland can work the same magic on you. Whether on the blustery seaside links or up in the highlands against the craggy mountains, the same depths and appreciation for the game will be instilled in you. There is nothing like it.

Playing in Scotland also will introduce you to some of the strangest, funkiest golf holes and courses you have ever experienced. By most American standards, you could call much of Scottish golf, "extreme golf". Blind shots, stone walls around greens, vertical-walled bunkers, it's all there. But once you understand that Scottish golf is all about life, it begins to make sense. Just as life is (all too often), a rather untidy affair — and even unfair — so too, is the golf there. As for the courses, while far from wall-to-wall manicured green perfection, they are real. The deeper you get into Scottish golf, the easier it gets to acknowledge that those funky bounces, good or bad, and those "unfair" lies are all merely parts of the game. At some point, you may even come to smile at the unexpected twists and turns the game can take (again, just like in life). In short, golf in Scotland is simply a wonderful elixir for the mind and soul of the golfer. You can't come away from it without gaining some greater understanding of what "it" is all about. Whatever "it" is.

On more practical terms, there are two ways that golfers "do" Scotland. The first is to use one of the many booking agencies that specialize in overseas golf holidays. Of course, while most of these companies are great when it comes to providing the whole nine yards, so to speak, the fact is, they don't necessarily come cheap. If you decide to go this route, shop around and get references.

The second method is arguably more fun, whether you're a Scotland rookie or a seasoned veteran: to go solo, or with a spouse, friend, or partner as a twosome, with little or no reserved tee times or booked hotels. I wholeheartedly recommend this for anyone who has already experienced Scotland via the first approach. You were coddled well enough then; now, going it on your own will deepen your education — of life and golf — in the land where it all began. Full disclosure: my own very first golf excursion to Scotland was solo, with only one secured tee time and one hotel reservation...and it was a most excellent adventure.

Going solo or as a twosome requires little more than planning where you want to play and a having a good roadmap of the country. There are plenty of wonderful books about getting around Scotland and its courses, but the standout is Golf in Scotland by American Allan

Ferguson (www.fergusongolf.com) that will give you all the help you need. One word of advice, though, that even Ferguson missed (and that I had to learn the hard way): after consulting all the maps and distances between destinations, it's best to double the estimated driving time, or at least add 50%. Trust me on this.

Second on my list of things to do after you turn 50 is to give back to golf. I'm going to assume that over the years, golf has given you a great deal, whether in friendship, memorable moments of beauty or excitement, or feelings of exultation after a great shot or round. So, for all that the game has afforded us, why shouldn't there be some obligation to give back something of ourselves?

Of course, you can always make a donation to your favorite golf charity, but for a couple of reasons, I have another idea: think about working with junior golf. First, by encouraging kids to learn golf, you are promoting the growth of our beloved game, as well as introducing the next generation to a pastime that will give them pleasure for the rest of their lives. The second reason I recommend working with junior golf is that it's a sure way to help recapture the simple, unadulterated joy of the game. There are few things as gratifying as the delight that lights up a kid's face after he or she stripes that first "perfect shot" down the fairway. For sure, if you're any kind of golfer, that ought to bring a smile of recognition to your face and a warm glow to your heart. As the man in the commercial says, "Priceless".

If you are looking for a program to support, call your local park district, YMCA, or check out the First Tee, a national organization begun in 1997 to help introduce golf and the positive values it promotes to youngsters of all backgrounds. While First Tee teaches golf, its true mission is to help develop character and good old life-enhancing values of honesty, integrity, and sportsmanship. It's a worthy concept; moreover, it's one that works: to date, there are over 150 First Tee chapters in the U.S., (that also means it's likely that there is one fairly close to you). For more information go to www.TheFirstTee.com. As for me, over the course of four decades playing golf, the most pleasure I have derived hasn't come from any great shot or score, but from knowing that I may have made some small difference by giving back to the sport.

And finally, number three, for those of us approaching, or who have passed, the big five-0: if you've already been to Scotland or are planning the trip, and if you also are giving back to golf, what you really want to know is this: is there anything you can do at this point to improve your own golf game? Of course, there may be a few golfers out there who are perfectly pleased with the state of their game, but most of us, I believe, at least occasionally wonder, "what if?"

If this sounds like you, then start by asking yourself if you are truly willing to commit to improving your game past 50. Don't be too quick to answer, either, because improvement doesn't come easily at any age. But, it can be accomplished. The answer is simple and it has always been out there: lessons. (What? You thought I was going to say a new driver? Get real.) I'm talking lessons from a PGA professional. Not from a magazine. Not from your uncle Harry who once broke 80, and definitely not from the chops in your weekly foursome. On the other hand, while wives can often see their husbands' swing flaws, the reverse never works. Don't even try.

Yes, the solution is lessons, and that means plural. If you do commit, the emphasis has to be on real change, not short-term gimmicks. I believe that a golfer must commit to at least a full season of lessons in order to see real improvement. The good news is that today's PGA professional is better schooled in the fundamentals of the modern golf swing. For those of us who learned golf in the 1960s, this may mean some clear changes. But don't be alarmed; if you are an astute golfer, you very well may become fascinated with the process as your understanding of the swing deepens. So get out there and enjoy — some of your best golf experiences are still ahead.

32

Throw a slow-dance party

**Marvin Gaye. Smoky Robinson. Frank Sinatra.
Invite a crowd of 50-somethings in to hear the sexiest
music ever, and feel the room heat up.**

BY NELSON GEORGE

Writer, filmmaker and cultural critic Nelson George was black
music editor of Billboard for seven years as well as a Village
Voice columnist He is the author of 10 books, both fiction
and non-fiction, including Where Did Our Love Go: The Rise
and Fall of the Motown Sound. His short film, To Be a Black
Man, featuring Samuel L. Jackson, has played in film festivals
around the world, as has his documentary, A Great Day in
Hip Hop.

O n Valentine's Day I decided to host a party. Not a
sweaty, up-tempo dominated throw down, but a gather-
ing fueled by the musical sensibilities of my youth. I
decided to a give an old school, red-light-in-the-basement
slow jam party. Initially it was a selfish notion. I've spent
much of my life writing about popular music but, as my
favorite artists either died or faltered, I craved the opportu-

nity to hear this music through high-quality speakers at a cool club.

I didn't realize how much the tradition of touch dancing and intimacy was a generational tradition until I started talking about the event. From adult women the idea elicited squeals of delight. From grown men it drew relieved smiles æ finally, a party they could attend and not look like the white guy from the Will Smith romantic comedy Hitch. Married couples saw it as an occasion to relive memories of passion long forgotten amidst stampeding kids and stacks of bills. From young singles, I sensed a satisfaction that they, finally, were being welcomed into the secret society of adulthood. I called it a Grown Folks party and, for all the attendees, that, as much as the music, was the attraction. Boomers, often portrayed as overgrown adolescents, found in this idea an acceptance of adulthood on their own terms.

The art of the slow jam, as practiced by masters such as Marvin Gaye, Smokey Robinson, and Frank Sinatra (you haven't lived until a DJ has mixed "Summer Wind" into "You Really Got a Hold On Me") suggest a lost world where you can still smoke in clubs, heads resting on shoulders and the warmth of two bodies becoming familiar. For those pushing or just pushed past fifty, this was a very familiar space. We didn't just dance this way at proms. The slow dance was a coming-of-age ritual for a great many Boomers, one fraught with anxiety, surprise, and opportunity. Who among us, except the most exceptional looking, have not felt the fear that no one will want to dance with us? And how great was the joy when someone did? And, finally, do you recall the wonder when you actually rocked in the same rhythm?

Growing up in New York, a city known for its sexuality, more than its sensuality, basement parties were a weekly event. Moreover, there was always time for slow dancing or grinding, a kind of vertical foreplay that I recall with great affection. But slow dancing was never just a black or urban thing. Down South, fans of country as well as soul and pop, were always at it.

There are a lot of things that define the Baby Boomer's relationship to popular music: the massive stadium concert, overt (and covert) political commentary, the concept of concept albums, AM top 40 radio, the transition from analog to digital, and the steady sexualizing of lyrics. There is a tendency to look at the Boomer's relationship to music only through the prism of rock's excess: LSD, Woodstock, indulgent guitar solos, unkempt jeans, couples wiggling to music several feet away from each other. From this point of view, all of us around 50 were hippies who later sold our souls for yuppie comforts. It is a convenient myth that both left-wing nostalgia merchants and right-wing pundits exploit to their advantage. But if you really look at the sweep of our musical experience, it's clear that this stereotype represents just one aspect of ourselves.

As much as we were part of a radical musical movement, we also harbored an intense romanticism. This yearning for emotional connection, fired by the challenges of war and social change, as well as our own personal journeys, runs through the work of the era's best-loved artists. When you consider the work of Sam Cooke, the Beatles, the Beach Boys, Bob Dylan, Smokey Robinson, Aretha Franklin,

Carole King, Stevie Wonder, the Eagles, Joni Mitchell, Willie Nelson, Bob Marley, Barry White, Paul Simon, the Bee Gees, and so many others, that desire to understand and express love is undeniable. Whether we categorize the music as soul, country rock, reggae, singer-songwriter, or disco, there is a common thread that unites them. And it is that shared sensibility that has produced the verses we hum, the choruses we sing, and the way we move our hips. Long after we stopped playing air guitar to Led Zep's "Whole Lotta Love" we still sing along in our car to Paul McCartney's "My Love" and Gaye's "Distant Lover."

At the slow jam party, people reacted with shouts when "Let's Get It On" came on, they slid closer when we surprised them with "Lay, Lady, Lay," and they looked into each other's eyes and swayed to "Let's Stay Together." The intro to songs, just a bass intro or a drum downbeat or a familiar voice singing a well-remembered opening line, produced murmurs. People got up out of their seats and pressed close. They weren't moved by this music simply out of nostalgia. They embraced it (and each other) because it's music that still speaks to an inarticulate yearning for a multileveled emotional connection, also known as love. At 50 the power of these songs to raise temperatures remains unabated. In fact, watching the adult crowd dance slowly, some mouthing the words in their lover's ears, I could see time has given this music more resonance, not less. All we need is love. Indeed. ☼

33

Lose your must-see list

The best way to be a tourist is to trash your list and dive right in.

BY PETER GREENBERG

The Travel Channel's chief correspondent, Greenberg is best known as the travel editor for NBC's Today Show, and also wrote the New York Times best-selling The Travel Detective series, which reveals the secrets to saving money on airlines, hotels, cruise lines and rental cars.

Turning 50 means it is time — if you haven't done so already — to jettison "the list." Now, don't deny you have one. We are a nation of list makers, especially when it comes to travel.

A destination is either on your list, or it's not. And, experience dictates that the list itself is ridiculous and misleading — literally. "I don't want to go there....it's not on my list." Not on your "list?" Let's start by what most people have on their list: Western Europe. Why? It's almost as if there's an entire generation of failed art history majors out there who desperately need to see Florence…at least once…so they can check it off their list.

Dump the list. It's only something to depart from. And if you insist on having a list, then the list must include every place you haven't been, every experience you haven't had. And then look at that list only once and repeat after me: I will not SHOULD on myself.

By the time I turned 50, travel had become synonymous with breathing. It's an involuntary act, and, like inhaling and exhaling, I travel to stay alive.

I don't plan to travel. I just travel, because I firmly believe that a plan, like that list, is only something to depart from. And therein lies the real beauty of travel — the idea, the opportunity, and the manifestation of being spontaneous without being irresponsible. To not only think, but live — literally — outside the box. And the key to the true serendipity of travel is to remove the word "later" from your vocabulary. Every time you use "later" in a sentence you either don't do it as well…or worse, you don't do it at all.

My father once told me that the key to life is not being smart, or beautiful, or right, or rich. The key, he explained, was in how you adjusted to what life gave you. And any kind of travel challenges you to adjust. It's how well you adjust, how fast you adjust, and how sensitively you adjust that makes the difference.

There has been a sea of change in the way people approach travel. It's no longer about the affordability of the destination. Instead, it's about the accessibility of the experience.

I was visiting Shanghai by cruise ship in 1984. As I

walked along the pier, heading towards a planned group bus tour of the city, a distinguished looking, well-dressed Chinese man who looked to be in his early 40s rode up to me on his bicycle. "You from the ship?" he asked in perfect English. "Yes," I replied, asking, "Do you live here?" He smiled. "All my life!" When I remarked about his mastery of English, he startled me. "Actually," he said, "this is really the first time I've been able to speak it since...1949." I never got on the bus. A few minutes later, 78-year-old Joe Cheng was taking me on one of the more remarkable journeys of my life — the history of Shanghai through his eyes.

A few years later I was touring one of the Philippine islands when we pulled into a hotel driveway. There, parked along the side, were 10 motorcycles. I asked who owned the bikes. One of the bellmen said he was a medical student, and the other medical students in Legaspi had formed a motorcycle club. I asked if I could rent one of the motorcycles. "I've got a better idea," he said. "Would you like for me to round up the other club members and take you for a bike tour?" An hour later, nine motorcyclists — plus me — were headed through a half dozen villages and towards the active volcano, a tour I'll never forget.

About 10 years ago, as I was exiting a Manhattan hotel, terribly late for the airport, I jumped into a yellow cab. "JFK," I ordered, along with directions, "head up Madison Avenue, turn right on 96th street, if the East River Drive is too crowded, then head up Third Avenue instead..."

The driver simply said in a thick Middle Eastern accent..."No, I'll take you a better way." A better way? Already stressed because I was so late, I was ready for a fight, or at least an argument. "Hey pal," I shot back. "I'm from New York. Just take me the way I want to go." But he was ready to take me that better way. "Let me ask you," he began. "What terminal do you want?" I told him Terminal Nine. "OK, we take my way, and if you're not at Kennedy in 26 minutes, the ride is free." Deal. The driver then took me on a route I had never been on in my life. And, shockingly, 22 minutes later, I arrived at JFK. The driver smiled. "You owe me," he laughed.

I asked his name. William. Where was he from? Alexandria, Egypt. But he lived in New Jersey. Was this his own cab? Yes. Then I had an idea. I took down his phone number and his cab number. And for the next eight years, William Megalla was my driver every time I came to New York. He drove my friends. He drove for my mother.

One day, while driving me into the city from the airport, he said he wanted to tell me some good news. His younger brother Billy was getting married, and his family wanted to invite me to the wedding. Would I go? Of course. Two months later, I was at that wedding….In Alexandria, Egypt. And that trip taught me a valuable lesson. In New York, William was just a cab driver. In Egypt, he was a god. The wedding took place at 10 p.m. inside King Farouk's palace on the Mediterranean. Five hundred celebrating Egyptian Coptics, and a guy named Greenberg.

So what are your new rules, now that you're turning 50? Spontaneity without being irresponsible. Going with the flow. Forgetting brochures. But never forgetting common sense.

Of course there is always the ticking clock as you get older. But travel after 50 slows that clock down as you speed up — it allows you to immerse yourself in a world of endless possibilities, a world where the debilitating borders of fear and misunderstanding become increasingly easy to ignore, and thankfully, a world where you can firmly embrace the notion that travel is a powerful force to build bridges, where every ride to the airport may not just be a short-term means to an end, but the start of a lifelong friendship. ☼

34

Go fishing

Some might say that 50 is too old to start fishing. Not so. It's never too late . . . , and when you fish, you'll discover a lot more than what is at the end of your line.

BY JAMES PROSEK

Called "the Audubon of the Fishing World" by the New York Times, Prosek is an artist and author who lives in Easton, Conn., and has been featured in such publications as People, Sports Illustrated, Sports Afield, and Life. His book, "The Complete Angler," was turned into an ESPN special, which won the Peabody Award.

Some might say that 50 is too old to start fishing. That is not so. If you have reached your 50s and have not yet exercised your primal instincts, then you have an exciting adventure in store and I believe that it will also offer you an opportunity to be more at peace with yourself and with the world.

I once wrote several years ago concerning the Compleat Angler, Izaak Walton's seminal work of 1653 on fishing as a contemplative recreation, that the book "is not about fishing, it's about life. Or rather, it is about fishing, but fishing is life." I would like to qualify that. One of the reasons that "fishing is life" is because it is part of our fabric. The act of stalking and capturing a fish, I'd like to think, is part of our development as cognitive beings. We are, after all — much as we try in day-to-day life to shake millions of years of evolution — hunter-gatherers.

There is evidence that Walton himself did not start fishing until he was forty, and he may be the single most influential fisherman that ever lived because his book was the first to outline the idea of predation as a recreation for contemplation. He adopted fishing into his life and found that many life lessons could be communicated metaphorically using fishing as the vehicle. The Complete Angler is instructional, a dialogue between a fisherman and a hunter where the fisherman ends up converting the hunter to his passion. A favorite passage in the book occurs when the hunter's line breaks on a big trout and he says "my rod is broken and I lost the fish." The fisherman then corrects him. "Nay, the trout is not lost, for you cannot lose what you never had." If you have the time and the patience, angler or not, I would recommend reading Walton's book.

As a young boy, without any instruction, I became obsessed with creatures in the pond on our dead end street. When my friend Stephen gave me a fishing rod at the age of nine, I was given my freedom. My mother had just left home and fishing became the only activity that made me feel secure and happy, in a time when things were anything but certain. Why did it feel so natural? Perhaps the hunter (and by this I don't mean bloodthirsty killer) within me had just been waiting for an opportunity to emerge.

Though modern angling is more angling for recreation than survival, the activity keeps our primal instincts fresh and alert. Many anglers today, including myself, practice catch and release. It may seem counter-intuitive to describe an angler as predatory if they let the fish go, but killing was never the only facet of predation. As hunters, we evolved with an admiration for our prey that made us more acute observers, which in turn made us better survivors. The earliest known drawings on cave walls were of animals that hunters were pursuing, an expression of that admiration that evolved in the throes of strategy and pursuit. Angling, perhaps, is a form of predation that plays up the aspect of admiration more than the goal of killing.

Izaak Walton called angling "a gentle art" — a phrase that does not bring to mind whacking things on the head, gutting them and eating them. Though Walton ate fish, he had the sensibility and admiration for the prey that a catch and release fisherman does. To Walton angling was spiritual. The author notes that the first followers of Christ, the apostles, were fishermen; humble observant men who followed peace. They were "fishers of men." Spirituality of some sort is an undeniable aspect of modern day fly-fishing. When you are out in nature, by the stream, you can lose all sense of time and space and become one with the river. The river is essentially an immortal eternity, always flowing, even while we remain mortal. So it's nice to look down and see our reflection in eternity.

If you have never angled, a good initial approach is through books. Other great angling works that convey the spirituality of the pastime are A River Runs Through It by Norman McClean, The River Why, by James David Duncan, and a small personal favorite of mine, The Year of the Trout by David M. Carroll. Reading any one of these stories will get you hooked and once you get into fishing it is hard to get out of it.

For a beginner fly fisherman, I recommend starting with trout fishing. Get a pair of chest-high waders, a nine foot long, five weight fly rod, a reel with five weight line, a box of assorted flies, a pair of polarized sunglasses for cutting down glare on the water, as well as eye protection, and if you can afford it, a guide to take you out.

You can learn a great deal from someone who knows how to fish. If you don't have the patience to learn how to cast a fly from reading books, watching videos, and experimenting, you can always find an instructor. Orvis Flyfishing Schools (www.orvis.com) have programs nationwide to teach you how to fish.

One of the greatest things about fishing is the places that it can take you. Once fishing is in your blood and you're ready to travel, I recommend a trip to one of two places: Alaska or New Zealand. You won't forget it, and you'll carry it with you the rest of your life. The author Robert Traver once wrote, "Trout will not, indeed, cannot live, except where beauty dwells." I've found that to be pretty much true, having chased trout from Connecticut to California, France to Mongolia. Wild trout require cool clean water to survive, so you usually find them in pristine wilderness settings.

Fishing is a sport you can do at home or abroad, alone or with friends, anywhere there is water — and you'll discover so much more than what is at the end of your line.

35

Check your "Turning 50" horoscope

Yep, it's still the Age of Aquarius: Now that you've hit 5-0, here's what to expect.

BY KAT LANE

Professional astrologer Kat Lane writes horoscopes and astrological features for numerous publications including Marie Claire, Mademoiselle, In Style, Mirabella, Flair, South Africa's Femina, and Latin American Cosmo. Kat's stellar insights are featured online at Swoon, Conde Nast's popular website where her interactive Love Matches continue to be the site's most "clicked-on" feature.

Think of the planets as celestial guides that help light our paths along a journey of self-discovery. Before there were metroplexes and plasma TVs to divert our attention, the ancients would pull up a rock and sit and watch real stars perform in the night sky. Over time, they began to notice a correlation between the movements in the heavens and our actions on earth. As above, so below. By putting us in sync with the natural rhythms and cycles of the universe, the study of Astrology can help us plan our lives more effectively. Why fight the tide when you can go with the flow? Of course, whether you're ready and waiting on the dock when your ship comes in, or passed out at the Tiki bar is entirely up to you. The stars can't force you to go anywhere; they can only point the way. Planning a move? Your retirement? The levitation of the Pentagon? Why not check out your cosmic map? Timing is everything. See what the stars have in store now that you've crossed the threshold into the fabulous 50s.

ARIES (3/21-4/20)

You've never looked — let alone acted — your age and there's no reason to start now. After all, 50 is just a number. And if you're like most rams, you're still loaded with brio and as eager as ever to take on new challenges. Here's one to test your mettle: Try completing just a few of the millions of projects you've started. You were blessed with great initiative, but with the attention span of a weather vane, you've always lacked follow-through. So while you're still able to travel in the fast lane, why not try crossing some "finish" lines?

TAURUS (4/20-5/20)

"I have, therefore I am" is the Taurean credo. If you are a typical "material bull," hitting your 50s may come as a shock when suddenly, the "beemer" ain't beamin', the Cristal's lost its fizz and the Armani doesn't seem to fit. When those creature comforts no longer satisfy, you need to think about tempering your raw materialism and tuning in to a higher plane. I'm not saying you have to turn into Shirley MacLaine and go out on a cosmic limb (although she is a Taurus), but it is time to discover the sacred cow within.

GEMINI (5/21-6/20)

Welcome to your 50s! In addition to getting your AARP card, you're now eligible to enroll in "The Big Picture," an exciting course that allows you to cultivate a global perspective and ponder new philosophies. Because you've perceived life in all its dizzying detail, you've never seen the forest for the trees (so many leaves, so little time). I think you'll find that adding this wide-angle view to your current perspective will prove both exciting and meaningful. You see, despite the old adage, you actually can have it both ways. Whoever said you couldn't obviously wasn't a Gemini.

CANCER (6/21-7/22)

Come out, come out wherever you are! The universe is prompting you soft-shelled crabs to vacate your safe havens and explore new terrain. The I-never-leave-my-zip-code types among you will find this terrifying. But don't get dyspeptic. No one is asking you to go claw to claw with a wild beast in Borneo. It's more likely you'll traverse the realms of the mind by say, taking a philosophy course, exploring different religions and/or exotic cultures. Think of this as an around-the-world-in-80-pages kind of trip. The best part for you homebodies? You have all of your 50s to accomplish this and you never have to leave your neighborhood.

LEO (7/23-8/22)

Remember how Superman could transform a lump of coal into a diamond by squeezing it in his fist? Now that you're 50, the cosmos is exerting similar pressure on you to do what you Sun gods were meant to do: shine. If you've been coasting on your charisma, it's time to test your talent. If someone else has been supporting your champagne tastes, it's time to cut that umbilical card (sic). You're ready to roar! I know you egoists will have no problem reflecting on your brilliance. You'll know you're making progress if you can do it without a mirror.

VIRGO (8/23-9/22)

You germ-phobes have a nasty reputation for disinfecting everything (and everyone) in sight. Why not turn this urge to purge on yourself and break free of these restricting stereotypes? Now that you've reached 50, the cosmos is granting you permission to throw in the towel and to stop mopping up everyone else's messes. If you do, you'll no longer be married to the miniscule, the menial and the mundane. You can reach for the stars and become the legend you were meant to be. All you have to do is promise to stop acting like Felix Unger on steroids.

LIBRA (9/23-10/22)

It's a cosmic paradox that you, the sign of equality and justness, so often sacrifice your own needs for peace-at-all-costs. The problem, my fair Libra, is not that you put the desires of others ahead of your own, but instead of you're own. How "fair" is that? Now that you're finally 50, the cosmos is cajoling you to drop the people-pleasing mask, the frilly inhibitions and the need to keep up appearances. Unleash your inner warrior! Let down your hair, pick up the sword and fight for your right to parity! You must do this to fulfill your Astrological destiny. It's called balance.

SCORPIO (10/23 -11/21)

The skeptic in you scoffs that I dare profess to know what you'll do in your 50s. You're right, I don't. All I can tell you is what energies are activating your chart and when. How, and with whom, you choose to manifest them is between you and your free will. That said, my hunch is you're going to become a lot more trusting and willing to purge yourself of old hang-ups, neuroses and obsessions. And, in the very near future you'll be radiating more faith, hope and cock-eyed optimism than a Sagittarius. It's already happening. You're reading this horoscope.

SAGITTARIUS (11/22-12/21)

You jet-setters are infamous for pulling geographics (escaping to faraway places) when things get too close for comfort. Seems the only baggage you're comfortable handling is carry-on. But scattering your attentions (and affections) keeps you from enjoying deeper experiences. Now that you're 50, the cosmos is exhorting you to explore some truly foreign territory — your feelings. Success here depends on your willingness to be profound and emotionally connected. In other words, acting as unlike yourself as possible. Finally, a challenge worthy of your adventurous nature!

CAPRICORN (12/22-1/19)

Life begins at 50 for you late-bloomers: you start out as old goats and end up as playful kids. Why? Because you were so overly responsible growing up. What other sign can boast that they put both parents through school with money from their paper routes? In recompense, the universe offers a second childhood just when you're smart enough to enjoy it. So throw your customary caution to the wind, explore your playful, creative side, kick up your heels and act like a "kid" again. After all, there's more to life than work.

AQUARIUS (1/20-2/18)

"Don't trust anyone over 30" was the rallying cry at the dawning of the Age of Aquarius. Even at 50, you mavericks can boast that you're still true to the spirit, if not the letter, of that sentiment. Here's your chance to prove it. The cosmos is challenging you to let go of some long-held, deeply entrenched ideals in order to realize a long-term goal. Now you can show the world how radical you truly are because this time, the "establishment" you're expected to overthrow is your own. So stay cool and remember: don't trust anyone under 30!

PISCES (2/19-3/20)

Strange visitors from another planet, you sensitive souls came to Earth with talents and abilities far beyond those of mere mortals. Sadly, Earth's bleak realities often crush your spirit, forcing some of you to drown your sorrows in designer martinis rather than realizing your artistic potential. Knowing the unfair burden placed upon you, the cosmos sometimes intervenes by emboldening you to manifest your wildest dreams. Turning 50 is one such time. So instead of plucking olives from your glass, try plumbing the depths of your creativity. I guarantee it will be a lot more fruitful.

Align yourself with your astrological destiny, and you'll increase the chance that the second half of your life will be out of this world!

36

Jump off a bridge

Every so often, it's good to defy your fears.

BY MARK FENTON

Mark Fenton hosts PBS' television series "America's Walking," and is a consultant to the University of North Carolina's Pedestrian and Bicycle Information Center. He also serves as an instructor in the walkable community workshop series of the Washington DC-based National Center for Bicycling and Walking, and wrote The Complete Guide to Walking for Health, Weight Loss, and Fitness (Lyons Press, 2001).

I t may not be the first idea you have when you turn 50, but I guarantee it will be the best: Go jump off a bridge.

I've come to the realization that most people don't jump off nearly enough bridges in their lifetimes. They stay on the safe side of the railing, doing comfortable things — things that will turn out exactly as they envisioned. But once you crest 50, it's absolutely time to take a little leap. Or maybe a big one.

I say this as a guy who has spent the bulk of his adult life trying to convince people to do more walking. "Get out and walk every day," I say. "It's good for you." Talk about boring. Talk about predictable. Talk about staying on the bridge. Nothing thrilling or unknown about walking.

Sure, walking is good for you — daily walking burns calories and helps you maintain a healthy weight as it tones your muscles, clears your head, and improves your mood. The Surgeon General says just 30 minutes of walking a day reduces your risk of chronic disease, and research confirms that regular walkers live longer, more independent lives. All great things, all great reasons to walk every day. But not really pushing the envelope.

That's why I had to jump off a bridge. Jumping helped me realize how right I've been all along about the walking. I can best explain it with a little story.

A few years ago I found myself at something of a mid-life crisis. I was leaving a job of many years at Walking Magazine, beginning work on a new PBS television series (about walking), and writing a book called The Complete Guide to Walking. Our children were growing up, and my career was decidedly, well, pedestrian.

My wife, Lisa, was getting nervous. She figured it was only a matter of time before I was gripped by the inevitable question: Gibson six string or Harley Davidson? So around my birthday in July, she took me out to our favorite local bistro to celebrate the person I had become. A person who talks about walking, eating your vegetables, and being healthy. I was appreciative, but unconvinced.

Returning to our neighborhood that evening we crossed a bridge that forms a gentle arc over a tidal estuary — a small river whose flow shifts with the tide. Sometimes the water is deep and swiftly flowing, sometimes a shallow trickle. As in many a coastal town, it's a summer rite of passage for the local kids to jump off the bridge into the current. Of course, you've got to time the tide and depth right, or you can end up with your feet sliced by razor-sharp barnacles. Or worse.

Two young girls in swimsuits were standing along the rail of the bridge. As they faced the water, their arms gripped the railing tightly, and both looked nervous about jumping. I heard a teenage boy — not the epitome of human good judgment — shout from the water below, "Go ahead, jump. It's deep enough, c'mon, let's go."

Instead of shouting the standard, "It's always funny until someone puts out an eye!" we looked at the kids. We looked at the tide. I looked at Lisa. She looked at me. I looked at her again. I said nothing, and then she said, "Okay, give me your wallet. Go on, just be careful."

So I handed her my wallet, pulled off my shirt and sandals, and scrambled over the rail. The girls were astonished, and the boy yelled up, "Hey mister, you jumpin'?" (Like I needed a "hey mister" on my birthday.) And we all did — we jumped safely, swam to the side, and were soon on our merry ways.

The incident was worth it just for the thrill of the jump and to see the looks on the kid's faces. But I've left the most important detail out of the story. How do you figure Lisa and I had traveled to dinner that evening? We'd walked, of course. We passed those girls on foot, moving maybe three miles an hour, not 30. We weren't separated from them by thousands of pounds of automotive steel and glass, but by just a foot or two.

And with that, I realized two very important things about the walking that I do and that I encourage others to do. First, it reminded me that living an active lifestyle is its own reward. I don't walk just to keep my weight down, my cholesterol in check, or my doctor off my back. I do it so when the chance comes to jump off a bridge, hike a new trail, or go mountain biking, I'll be young enough at heart and fit enough in body to actually do it!

It's as simple as this: Being a walker assures that you won't miss your own bridge-jumping chance when it comes. Your bridge may be hang gliding or it may taking a walking tour in France, but you won't have to pass it up if you stay active and fit. Whatever your plunge, get out for a walk, every single day, and when the chance comes to jump off a bridge, jump. You never know where you'll land. But I guarantee it will be a better place. ☀

37

Read the classics

Want to have time to re-read the good stuff? Stop reading all of the bad stuff.

By HAROLD BLOOM

Bloom is Sterling Professor of Humanities at Yale University, Berg Professor of English at New York University, a former professor at Harvard. He holds honorary degrees from the universities of Rome and Bologna. His more than 20 books include Shakespeare: The Invention of the Human, How to Read and Why, and Where Shall Wisdom Be Found? He lives in New Haven, Conn.

First of all, from the vantage point of 74, 50 doesn't seem much different than 20. But, although the benefits of learning are limitless, time is not. I've been saying for years that the real reason one should read the canonical, the traditional, and better works, is that, finally, there is less and less time. As I get older, I seem to be busier than I was the year before.

In a sense, learning can be considered a race against the clock, because there will never be enough time even if you read all your life, as I have. But obviously, you can't do nothing but read your whole life. Schopenhauer, a great book man, warns against that, and Emerson who also aspired to read everything, issued a warning. He says, rather beautifully, "Reading is for a scholar's idle hours."

A teacher of literature at 74 years old is rather like one of those big league baseball pitchers, particularly if the teacher has been æ as I think it's fair for me to say I was, and I hope still am æ of a certain power and proficiency. The rare pitchers like Mr. Randy Johnson and Mr. Roger Clemens continue to be power pitchers at what many people consider middle age. Most pitchers who are still pitching into their mid-40s and have done it well æ and there are a few of them in the big leagues æ have become pitchers of a very different kind.

In some ways, like the baseball pitchers, I've improved as a teacher. (Maybe not my temperament, but my energy level is certainly different.) I used to go into the classroom with fire and passion and so much expressionistic drive that I didn't really give the students an opportunity to answer my questions or hold discussions. Now I'm much more patient. My happy moments in the classroom come more frequently than they used to. When a discussion ensues, I sometimes sit, listening to the way it develops and grows. I don't think that would have happened back in the days when I was, as it were, too much of a power pitcher.

No age is too old to learn. To read that which is most worth reading can take you down a profound path. I have students in my classes æ "old dogs" of 50, 60, or even 70 years old — and I've seen them learn. But unless one has developed aesthetic and intellectual standards, and some sense of what is wise or not, then an ocean of information is not necessarily a good thing. The challenge is to know what to learn and how to learn it. To learn to cultivate the ability to judge the truth of information is a major factor. And if one doesn't read and remember the very best that has been written, then they'll never learn how to think critically, because thinking depends upon memory, and without memory, one can't think.

There are books that, if one reads them through and gets to know them well enough, are a classroom in and of themselves. They offer pleasure, of course, the pleasure of insight, among others. Shelley defines the sublime, which means the highest kind of experience one can have in reading, as learning to give up easier pleasures for the more challenging ones. Obviously Proust is a more difficult pleasure than most of the reading one picks up today.

Reading and learning prepares us for how to live, and that means living up to the very end. My own interpretation, which my friend Tony Kushner is kind enough to have said he picked up from me and used as the cornerstone of Angels In America, is a translation of the biblical Blessing (with a capital B) as being "more life." Reading, as I view it, is a great Blessing and it will potentially give one more life.

At one point in my book Where Shall Wisdom Be Found?, I quote, with great joy, a marvelous remark of Montaigne, "Don't bother yourself with preparing to learn how to die. When the times comes, you'll know how to do it well enough."

Section Eight

WATCHING THE
BIG PICTURE

38

Don't go off the deep end

It took leaving his wife, losing his job, and getting lymphoma to show this sailor who — and what — really mattered to him.

BY GARY JOBSON

Gary Jobson is a world-class sailor, television commentator, and author of 14 sailing books, the latest being Championship Sailing. He has won many championships including the America's Cup with Ted Turner in 1977, the infamous Fastnet Race, and has led expeditions to the Arctic, Antarctica and Cape Horn. Jobson has been ESPN's sailing commentator since 1985, winning Emmy for his coverage of yachting at the Olympics in South Korea in 1988.

Jobson has given lectures around the world over the past 30 years and is editor-at-large of Sailing World and Cruising World magazines. Gary was part of the broadcast team that covered sailing events at the 2004 Summer Olympics in Athens, Greece. He is a recipient of The Leukemia & Lymphoma Society's 2004 Spiral of Life award.

I laugh when people say 50 is just a number. It wasn't for me. Attaching the number 50 to my name felt like a major milestone. All at once I had a sense of accomplishment, a feeling of freedom, and a sudden license to do things never before contemplated. In a word, I went "nuts" at a time when my health was perfect, my family life secure, and my business thriving. It was easy to take it all for granted. Turning 50 made me feel entitled to change my universe.

There had been bigger birthday celebrations. My surprise 40th party attracted many friends, family members, and business associates from across the country. Over 200 people were there. It was nice. During that decade I watched my kids grow up, my reputation in the world of sailing advance, and my net worth shift from substantial debt to significant assets.

With all this good fortune, the obvious question would be why change anything? But in the three years after I turned 50, my world did change, for the worse, at every level.

Perhaps it was because I was in a rut. Home life had become routine. My wife of 26 years, Janice, started a new career as a teacher. She was busy, had her own sense of independence, and still looked after three active daughters. I felt I had become a low priority. The girls spent increasing amounts of time with their school, sports and social lives, so I too went off in my own direction. In 1999 alone I wrote 50 articles, one book, gave 63 lectures, produced 25 television shows, attended 42 board meetings, traveled 250 days, and received the Nathanael G. Herreshoff Award, the highest honor in American sailing for my contributions to the sport.

It was exhilarating!

Our tight family was shooting off in five very different directions. My eldest daughter Kristi was preparing to attend Harvard. Twins Ashleigh and Brooke excelled in their respective sports, water polo and lacrosse. So, after a low-key 50th birthday party, I took our busy family sailing in Maine and Canada for a month on a special chartered 56-foot sailing yacht. But I had the rumbling feeling my family didn't really want to be there. The cruise was ambitious, rarely stopping at a marina, and I became frustrated when the inevitable squabbles bubbled up. When it was over, everyone seemed relieved to return to their regular schedules. I left for Sydney, Australia to cover the Olympic sailing competition for NBC. When I returned from the fast-paced Games, my wife and daughters were comfortably ensconced in their daily routine. I felt like a "$10 extra" in a movie, neither needed nor appreciated.

Looking at some old pictures triggered a trip down memory lane and I began reminiscing about an old girlfriend with whom I had raced small sailboats and shared an on-and-off romance between the ages of 16 and 22. When we net again, although we clearly weren't 16 anymore, the hours spent recalling our shared past led to more meetings and we eventually left our respective families. She too had just turned 50.

The next two years were a dizzying whirl of travel, television shows, speaking engagements, sailing, and the excitement of a new life. But deep down I didn't feel good about it. The slow divorce and the pain I was causing ripped me apart. And the thrill of the new began to wane.

Then without warning, ESPN, my most important client of 16 years, decided to stop covering sailing, disastrous for me both financially and emotionally. My star began to fade. Or so I thought. The last major event we covered on ESPN was the 2003 America's Cup. We had the best coverage of the worst sporting event. After the American boats were eliminated early, the American public didn't care. Plus, the host New Zealand race officials kept delaying the race for days, waiting for favorable wind (for their team). The debacle understandably upset ESPN executives; the viewing audience abandoned the Cup in droves.

Leading up to the Cup I had gone a little loony. I stopped getting haircuts and got an earring. To my exceedingly polite friends, it must have looked like a massive midlife crisis.

And in the midst of all this turmoil I started to feel ill. I began coughing uncontrollably. At night, I woke up drenched from sweat. Red blotches appeared on my arms and legs. I lost a lot of weight, was chronically tired, and every night I vomited for hours. But I kept working. After the America's Cup, I set off on a 60-city lecture tour. It was hard. I was able to deliver the lectures, but everything else from travel to eating was a hardship.

After three doctors, two prostate biopsies and countless blood tests, no one could figure out the problem, or a solution. It got worse. By my 23rd talk in Cleveland I could barely stand. A doctor in the audience said I didn't look good and invited me to his clinic the next morning. After five hours of tests, he said, "I don't know what's wrong with you, but you are very sick and need to go home." Just to be contrary, I gave presentations for three more nights before returning home to a little condo I had in Baltimore. It was lonely there. My old girlfriend visited infrequently. A sailing pal of mine who was a doctor arranged a series of tests that went on for 10 days, culminating — finally—in a diagnosis: lymphoma, cancer of the lymph nodes.

It took six rounds of chemo, surgery, high-dose chemo, a stem cell transplant, and 16 months before I was moving around comfortably.

Overwhelming worldwide support flooded in in many forms: e-mails, letters, visits.   Janice, whom I had left, was there for me on a regular basis. Years before, she had been an oncology nurse and knew the challenges I faced.

I was constantly surprised by the many setbacks I experienced; it seemed for every two steps forward, there were more steps back.

After nearly a year of endless procedures, a stem cell transplant and unbelievable pain, depression set in and I could feel myself slipping away. I couldn't walk. I was constantly drugged. But as I lay there, I thought: "I'm not done yet. I wasn't ready to check out. I felt an inner spark through all the confusion of drugs and pain, that I could still be constructive and productive. If I could get through this, I resolved to repair my marriage, work only on meaningful projects, embrace the kids' emerging independence, and savor good health.

It was a turn-around. During my darkest days I wrote Championship Sailing with my longtime assistant Kathy Lambert.   Every day, chipping away at the book project, I was able to visualize my years of racing sailboats. I thought through all the techniques I learned and got them down on paper. Writing was good therapy and enabled me to chart a course that would get my health, and my life, back on track.

While sitting idle for months trying to get well, I calculated the total number of races I'd been in — about 5,000. There were so many rewards to this: the freedom spent on the water; sailing the waters off every continent and seeing the world from this vantage point (quite different than taking a short trip as a tourist), it can't help but expand your worldview and your capacity for understanding; getting to know people who shared my passion for sailing. I got to race a lot with very successful people — leaders in their fields, pioneers like Ted Turner, the Duke of Edinburgh, the King of Spain — working with them gave me an opportunity learn from their expertise as well as offer mine. Sailing was the vehicle that provided valuable lessons that sustained me through the most difficult period of my life.

I'm now halfway between 50 and 60. At the moment my cancer scans are clean. I'm living happily with Janice, our girls are off to college, and my business is back on track.

It's hard to know if stress can cause an illness, but I do know that we all make our own choices. Certainly, windshifts will come along the way, but clear thinking and analysis will help overcome every problem. You can be on the water, with the wind at 10 mph and the sun's out, and an hour later in harsh conditions with the wind blowing 50 mph. In a tough sailing race you try to level off when all hell breaks loose. In races I have usually been the tactician, the calm one who keeps things steady. A tactician looks at everything, constantly predicting what happens next, which makes everyone else calm. You can't be in the middle of a race thinking about where you've been, you have to think about where you are now and where you want to go. If I didn't have that background, I don't think I'd have been able to turn things around. Move on to the rest of the race. If you dwell on the mistakes you've made, you'll never get back on track. Oddly, five years later and back on course, I have few regrets about my actions and circumstances.

My lesson is to savor what is good in life, adapt to change, and never give up trying to be better. With that attitude, you do move up in the fleet. For me, 50 is not just a number. ☀

39

Let your life flash before your eyes

You're turning 50. Accept it, and make the experience worthwhile.

BY ROBERT THURMAN, PH.D.

Robert Thurman is a scholar and the Jey Tsong Khapa Professor of Indo-Tibetan Buddhist Studies in the Department of Religion at Columbia University. He is the best-selling author of over ten books, a former Tibetan Buddhist monk, President of Tibet House in New York City, a close personal friend of His Holiness the 14th Dalai Lama, and father of five children including the Hollywood actress, Uma. He is a frequent lecturer at venues around the world and in 1997 was chosen by Time Magazine as one of the 25 most influential Americans.

When you reach 50, it is an ideal time to think about the meaning of life in a stronger way because the meaning of death becomes really important. To understand the meaning of life, I think you have to confront and deal with the meaning of death.

Life has one kind of meaning if you think of it solely as your physical life, from birth to death. Your consciousness, your sense of being, of subjective presence, is totally identified with your body and brain. When that body and brain are destroyed at death, then you absolutely and forever cease to exist. Living in this context conveys a certain meaning.

But, if what you really are is a soul that goes into future existences in some form or another, then this philosophy of life has another kind of meaning. Particularly if that soul is controlled by a deity, and, depending on your belief system, your adherence to a particular religion. In the Buddhist religion, your soul is a product of your own mind and your physical and verbal actions — your evolutionary actions (your karma); it is your own actions that determine what happens to you.

The Buddhist view is that you make yourself, or unmake yourself, all the time. If you behave well and cultivate your good qualities, they will intensify and you'll be better. You'll be happier. You'll be a better person. And if you let yourself go, you'll be worse. That belief becomes the meaning of life. That you do more good things and become a better being.

Think of it as lifting weights. If you lift weights, you get a strong bicep. Nobody awards you with the bicep from lifting the weights. You get it by lifting the weights — it's the "doing." It changes your arm muscle. Similarly, your moral muscle, your happiness muscle, your wisdom muscle, intelligence muscle — these things are all changed by what you do with your body and mind.

In my life, I lost an eye at 20. Some people would think

that was a terrible, horrible thing. Even I probably felt that way at the time. But it was actually lucky in the long run. Because, even at 20, it gave me a taste of mortality. You normally don't get that opportunity — you dance around, drive too fast, ride your motorcycle, whatever. In America anyway, many behave mindlessly and carelessly. But it made me realize that life is something you take seriously. What am I doing here? What is the point? What should I try to get out of it? It intensified my quest for spiritual meaning.

Your sense of your own mortality can intensify the quest to know what the world is. Just like when you travel somewhere, you want a guidebook. You look it up: this church was built then, and that monument was created then. Napoleon slept here, and so on. When you know more about it, you get more out of it.

So why wouldn't that apply to the fundamental situation of life on this planet? How could it not be important to really know what's going on? Certainly, we can just live by the myths of others. Many people choose that route: blind faith. We rely on the authority of scientists with their Big Bang, their double-quad experiment, their quantum quarks, whatever theories they come up with. We do whatever we're conditioned to do, without exploring for ourselves. Personally, I'm not satisfied with that. When traveling, don't most of us investigate the best airline, the best hotel, what clothing to bring, what language is spoken? So why not investigate what is the best way to be?

If you haven't explored some of these ideas, 50 is a good time to start. It isn't just about aging. It's what people learn from their years of experience. You're going to have to turn

50 anyway, and there's no way out of it. It's up to you to make it into something worthwhile. Perhaps that involves changing your habits, so that you can enjoy moments.

Of course, it is immensely beneficial if you have used your time to develop wisdom and friendliness; if you've realized that the really important things in life are friendships and kindness, that you've been most happy when you've helped others to be happy. Look back and remember the moments of your life that were the great moments — moments when you were caring for another and forgot about yourself. Those were your great moments. When your Self felt satisfied.

You can turn the fact that you may not be as limber or as spry as you once were into an advantage. You can be of benefit to others. Because of your age, you now have some authority with the young. You can help them have a good life. Don't spoil them too much, but don't be too hard with them either. Help them find a good path — doing so can make you happy.

If you think, "Hey, what do I get out of being 50?" you're going to be miserable, because it will not be enough. But if you ask, "Well, now I am 50. How can I use that well, to have a better moment?" Then you might find that turning 50 is an enriching experience. Live moment to moment. Help others more. Have more fun with them, and appreciate what is of value.

Regrets can be a great teacher too. People often find themselves making amends on their deathbed. You've got the opportunity to fix things now, when you reach a milestone like 50, so try to anticipate those future regrets and deal with them now. Then you won't have a bunch of them with you on your deathbed.

There are certain truisms that resonate for a reason, one of which comes from the great doctor and author Elisabeth Kübler-Ross, who said she had never met anyone on his or her deathbed who regretted not having spent more time at the office. People do regret not having spent more time with their loved ones. Not having read more poems. Not having looked at more sunsets. So why not, when you have time to act on these realizations, be more realistic about life, and use those lessons.

Life is not just survival. People say when they're dying, or when they have a near-death experience, that their life flashes before their eyes. Turning 50 is a good time to let that happen, even if you live another 50 years, because time is relative and it will seem like a flash before you're there anyway.

As old Carlos Castaneda used to say, take death as your advisor and realize how precious moments are, how precious the now is, and live it better.

40

Read the Torah

**You don't have to be Jewish to tackle the Torah.
Turns out Moses has things to say that are relevant
to everyone.**

BY RICHARD SIEGEL

Richard Siegel is the Executive Director of the National
Foundation for Jewish Culture, an organization dedicated to
strengthening Jewish identity in America through the arts
and humanities. He is the co-editor of The Jewish Catalog
(JPS), the insider's guide to the Jewish "counterculture" of
the late 1960s, as well as The Jewish Almanac (Bantam Books)
and the Commission Report on the Future of Jewish Culture
in America (NFJC, 2002).

ere are my assumptions: A. If you are Jewish, you probably had a bar mitzvah or bat mitzvah when you were
13, but since then you've rarely been voluntarily inside
a synagogue. You know that Jews are called "The People of
the Book," but you've never read the book and don't really
know whether this means one particular book or books in
general.

B. If you are not Jewish, you are curious as to what

exactly entitles the Jews to the sobriquet, "People of the Book," particularly given A.

C. If you are approaching 50, or are over 50, you might finally have some time to read books more challenging than summer novels.

So first things first.

There is, in fact, one book, and it is called the Torah. The only problem is that the Torah is a scroll, not a book, and the English translation of it is generally titled The Five Books of Moses. So the book we are talking about really contains five books and isn't even a book itself.

In any event, this is THE book that people mean when they talk about the "People of the Book." The reality, however, is that most Jews have never read it in its entirety, in spite of the fact that a portion of it is read in synagogues each week in sequential order and on an annual cycle. This means that if you had been going to synagogue regularly on Saturday mornings, you would have heard the Torah recited in its entirety at least 37 times since you were 13.

Why isn't it read more? Because this book — the Torah, the Pentateuch, the Five Books of Moses — is intimidating. It bears the weight of being the most studied, poured-over, commented-on book in the history of the world. It is the fundamental text of two of the three Western religions and the jumping off place for the third. How could a non-scholar, a non-professional, a non-cleric, hope to understand it or its context, its history, its theology?

The reality, however, is that it is pretty straightforward and, for the most part, clearly written. There is no reason not to just pick it up and start reading and finish when you reach the end. In fact, this should be the way it is read, not just for the first time, but at least once every five years.

So pick up a copy of the Torah and just start reading, preferably in Hebrew. There's nothing like the Torah in Hebrew, but not that many people know Hebrew, or at least know it well enough to read the Torah in its original version. If you don't, you are going to have to use a translation.

Fortunately, there are a number of good translations from which to choose, and I am just referring here to Jewish translations. There is no universally accepted standard translation; all translations differ, and how they differ is a function of the premises and biases of the translators. In other words, translations are also commentaries that reflect the particular perspectives of the translator. The following are four contemporary translations, all well-regarded and widely used:

1. The JPS Bible. The all-time best seller of the Jewish Publication Society of America; for a long time, this was the standard English translation used in synagogues and schools, particularly in the Conservative movement. It is based on solid scholarship and was newly re-translated as recently as 1985. It is good, reputable, and readable.

2. The Schocken Bible, otherwise known as the Fox Translation, in tribute to its translator, Everett Fox. Published as The Five Books of Moses in 1995, this is an exquisitely rendered translation, which tries to capture as much of the sound and rhythm of the original Hebrew language as possible. Interestingly, this is actually a translation of the German translation prepared by the great philosophers Martin Buber and Franz Rosensweig.

3. The Stone Edition, also known as the Art Scroll Torah. Published in 1996, this is a scholarly translation based on the Orthodox perspective. This has become a well-accepted translation, even in Reform and Conservative contexts, partly because of its attractive layout and design.

4. The Alter Translation. Just recently published by Norton in 2004, this translation by Berkeley literary scholar Robert Alter is a delight to read, based on brilliant scholarship – both literary and Biblical – and written with beautiful style.

Each of these, by the way, also comes with commentaries, some as part of the volume, some published separately. For this first read, you should ignore the commentary. Just start reading. Read a little each day, a couple of chapters, and pretty soon you will have read through it.

Actually, this is not as easy an instruction as it might seem, because you are very likely to be drawn into one thing or another — to get stuck on a word, an idea, a story. Certainly, some of it will probably be familiar to you, if only through osmosis from general society. The Ten Commandments, for instance, or the story of Creation. Some of it, however, will probably be startlingly new, even surprising. There are some pretty odd stories told in there, and even some of the familiar ones have twists which you might not have remembered or learned. So it may be hard to stick to the reading without going off and following one string or another. But keep at it, push through, and keep reading to the end. Write down a list of questions if you want to go back to them later.

Okay, you've read the Torah. Now what? Eat. One of

the ways that Judaism reinforces the pleasure of books is by associating reading with food. Children are introduced to the Hebrew Aleph-bet by licking honey off the letters. For adults, when we finish a book, we have a festive meal. So invite some friends and have a dinner party. At some point during the evening, however, you should give a book review. Talk about your most recent read, The Five Books of Moses, as you would the new Philip Roth book, the new Tom Clancy novel, or the new movie that you saw, for that matter. What do you think about the characters, plots, structure, language, and messages? It would be even better if everyone in the group had read it, maybe with different translations, because then you could have a good argument. (For any non-Jewish readers, it's important to understand that argumentation is a key element of Jewish life. If something doesn't generate an argument, it pretty much doesn't exist.) But even if you are the only one who has read it, it is very likely that your book review will stimulate an interesting interchange.

What's next? Maybe nothing. Put the book to the shelf, or pass it on someone else, and enjoy the sense of achievement and satisfaction of having finally read the fundamental text of Western Civilization. For at least the next year, you will be able to strike up cocktail party conversations with a line like, "I was reading the Torah recently, and found something interesting..."

If, on the other hand, your interest is piqued, there is a world of follow-ups. First of all, buy the other three translations. Then pick one and start reading from the beginning all over again. Only this time, when you get to a word, sentence, idea or passage that raises a question in you, look up how the others translate it. Here, as an example, are the first three verses of Genesis as translated in the four editions:

JPS:

When God began to create heaven and earth — the earth being unformed and void, with darkness over the surface of the deep and a wind from God sweeping over the water —God said, "Let there be light"; and there was light.

Fox:

At the beginning of God's creating of heavens and earth,

when the earth was wild and waste,

darkness over the face of Ocean,

rushing-spirit of God hovering over the face of the waters —

God said: Let there be light! And there was light.

Art Scroll:

In the beginning of God's creating the heavens and the earth — when the earth was astonishingly empty, with darkness upon the surface of the deep, and the Divine Presence hovered upon the surface of the waters — God said, "Let there be light," and there was light.

Alter:

When God began to create heaven and earth, and the earth then was welter and waste and darkness over the deep and God's breath hovering over the waters, God said, "Let there be light." And there was light.

Now see if there are any notes or editorial comments about the passage. In so doing, you will find that the text has depth. There are multiple readings. There are multiple ways of understanding even the simple meaning of the text.

You are now "studying" the Torah, not just reading it. You have now entered into the "Sea of Torah." Enjoy the process, and remember to have a meal each time you finish the book. ☀

41

Time to start unlearning

Fifty is a great time to forget everything you ever thought you knew about God — and start over.

BY FATHER JOSEPH KELLY, S.J.

Father Joseph Kelly is the youngest of seven children born in County Offaly, Ireland. He joined the Jesuits in 1949 and after 14 years of study, was ordained. He took his undergraduate degree in English language and literature in 1954 at University College, Dublin. He came to the United States in 1965 for post-graduate studies at Cornell and Loyola. He served as chaplain at St. Peter's College in NJ for 20 years. In 1993, he joined St. Malachy's, The Actors Chapel in NYC as Parochial Vicar, as well as on-call chaplain to St. Vincent's hospital, where he serves to this day.

Russell Baker once wrote a whimsical article about founding a "University of Unlearning." In it, he wrote, the more "facts" one was able to jettison the better. The degree would be a "Non-Bachelor of Un-Arts" and would be given to those who clearly manifested their ignorance of factual knowledge. Being a priest, this naturally made me think of the Catholic Church.

I looked at the word "unlearn." I thought to myself, that's something I need to do. Gradually I began to go back over much of what I was taught as a "practicing Catholic" and started the painful, but fruitful, process of "unlearning." I took a good look at all I had been taught about God, sin, hell, sex, purgatory and, most of all, what I hadn't been taught about love. I suddenly had the novel idea to use my God-given intelligence and its attendant right to question, believing that God's benign and loving Spirit would guide me as I tried to free myself from some of the lopsided legacies and false images that were passed off to me as "religion" or, worse still, "the will of God."

So much of what has been instilled in me, in all Catholics, is solely church imposed, mere human dogma, always bristling with eternal sanctions of hellfire. There was so little talk of love, so much more talk of rules and regulations. Since I've passed 50, I look over my amassed "knowledge" and find that "unlearning" much of this material, to get at the underlying principles, to get to the heart of the matter, is the clearest path to God. A Jesuit spiritual author once wrote "the longest journey in the spiritual life is from the head to the heart." "Unlearning" is an important step on that journey.

Of course, even the beginning of this journey is immediately problematic. You see, I was born with Original Sin on my soul. That gets me off to a pretty poor start. If I died without ever being baptized, then my fate, and that of all poor pagan babies for that matter, is eternally sealed — hellfire forever. I was born with what the Irish catechism called a "propensity to evil." Nobody ever mentioned that I might have a "propensity to good." In 43 years as a Jesuit priest, I have performed many baptisms. As I look into the innocent eyes of a baby, is it my church or my God that compels me to think, "come here you little bundle of 'propensity to evil' and God will straighten out your immortal soul"? Was I born as some kind of "sloppy seconds" like a faulty garment or piece of cracked pottery? Clearly, a bit of "unlearning" might be beneficial.

Let's have a look at the obligation to go to Mass on Sunday. Rather a mixed message. On the one hand God affirms his unconditional love for us. On the other He tells us "you've got to come and see me once a week, as well as on the special Holy Days of Obligation. If you don't come, and you don't have a good reason why not, then that's a mortal sin, and you know that means that hellfire for all eternity again." How does one RSVP to that sort of invitation? Would you go regularly to visit someone based on the fear of what would happen if you didn't? Would a friend or lover issuing that kind of ultimatum be indicative of a healthy relationship? What kind of image of God are we left with? Looks like more "unlearning" might help here.

In a book I once read and enjoyed, Good Goats: Healing Our Image Of God, the authors address God's image problem in this manner, asking, "do you see God as your prosecuting attorney, or your defense attorney?" Our answer to that question tells us a lot about how we see God — and love. Is my God one who truly loves me and will stand up for me, or one who is only bent on judging me, twice no less, at the Particular Judgment and the General

Judgement. The question then becomes, do we have some serious "unlearning" to do about God?

The dangerous "allies" of our whole way of thinking are of course Fear and Guilt. Years in the confessional have revealed the sad soul searching and gut-wrenching worry suffered by so many Catholics, "did I...didn't I? I'm not sure Father, but I'm telling you just in case." Neuroses flourish. As the poet John Milton said, "The hungry sheep look up and are not fed." People agonize over relationships, ordinary situations, moral decisions, forgetting both God's love and the truth that would set them free. Such attitudes still persist, people still need to be taught how to love and be loved. Sermons are still boring; the message of God's love still needs to be explained; people still need to be lifted up, reassured, and helped to turn and face a smiling God.

This leads to "unlearning " about the church. Many are angry at a church that has left them confused and bewildered. Ecclesiastical power was abused, scandals surfaced, and the tragedy now is that for many Catholics the church, which could be such a source of spiritual support, is seen as largely irrelevant. The voices of those who do have words of hope and love are not listened to. Because, too often we set out to make people feel guilty, and we are now reaping the fruit of what we sowed.

So, finally we must ask how one goes about the "unlearning" process. I think it will involve loving and that might mean risk and disruption. By the time we are 50, perhaps we are wise enough, or have enough experience to start making distinctions between rules and the principles underlying them. We have to try to see our God in a new and liberating light. Going to Sunday Mass should be something we want to do, not something we have to do. The Sacrament of Confession should be an encounter with a loving and compassionate God who knows our weaknesses long before we try to express them. Our faith should be something God has given us to make us free, and not a source of constant constraint. The ultimate goal is to love and be loved. This sounds so trite, so easy to say, so hard to do, but I think the person who loves and is loved will still always be "unlearning," because such a one is open and resilient, aware of one's weakness and fallibility.

In his wonderful little book The Four Loves, C.S. Lewis writes about the dangers of closing one's heart; such dangers can also apply to closing one's mind. "To love at all is to be vulnerable. Love anything, and your heart will certainly be wrung and possibly be broken. If you want to make sure of keeping it intact, you must give your heart to no one, not even an animal. Wrap it carefully around with hobbies and little luxuries, avoid all entanglements; lock it up safe in the casket or coffin of your selfishness. But in that casket — safe, dark, motionless, airless — it will change. It will not be broken; it will become unbreakable, impenetrable, irredeemable. The alternative to tragedy, or at least the risk of tragedy, is damnation. The only place you can be perfectly safe from the dangers and perturbations of love is hell."

Strong words which make us realize our dependence on the grace of God who wants us to be more than we are, or more than we think we can be. This means a commitment to the possibly painful but ultimately freeing and most important, loving process of "unlearning." What better time than your 50s to matriculate from Russell Baker's University!

42

Live your faith and enjoy the world

Islamic tradition says we should live as if we're going to live forever, and die tomorrow. A Muslim cleric weighs in on how to strike this tricky balance.

BY FAROQUE KHAN, M.D.

Dr. Faroque Khan is the spokesman and president of the Islamic Center of Long Island, he is a Master at the American College of Physicians, and is the author of three books including Story of a Mosque in America. He has served as advisor on the television program Our Muslim Neighbor with God Squad hosts Rabbi Marc Gellman and Msgr. Tom Hartman. Dr. Khan is the recipient of numerous awards, among them, the American College of Physicians Laureate Award, the American Federation of Muslims from India's Excellence Award, and Newsday's 2004 Everyday Hero Award.

For Muslims, it is the 40th year that holds special significance, so by 50 you will have had ten more years to reflect.

Muslims believe that we are in this world for a short period of time and the real life, the eternal life, is the hereafter. Everyone will die, then there will be a resurrection, a day of accountability. And on that day, God decides whether one goes to Heaven or Hell. A Muslim's goal is to aim for the Heaven. How does one do that? The guidance is in the Quran (Koran), which is the Scripture we believe in. We believe in the Old Testament, the New Testament, and that the Quran is the final Testament.

Our faith instructs us that you have to do for your neighbors what you would do for yourself. Now, the neighbor is not just the guy down the street; the neighbor is also the man in Indonesia/Somalia/Palestine who has no home right now. These are the issues that will be examined by God on the Day of Judgment. God says, "I left you in this world. I gave you good health. I gave you resources. What did you do with them? Did you follow the instructions? Or did you behave as though this world is the only life; there's nothing else to look forward to?"

Those instructions are about sharing and caring — the Ten Commandments basically. Our "instructions" in the Quran are an extension and refinement of the Judeo-Christian tenets, a follow-up on them, if you will. There are some differences with Christian beliefs; for instance we believe Jesus was a great prophet (peace be upon him), but not that he was the physical form of God — beyond that, the beliefs are really much the same. Do for your neighbor what you would do for yourself. Love thy neighbor.

Islamic tradition holds that a human being is a very special creature endowed with intellect, choice, and free will.

At the same time, there is an awareness that we are dependent upon a higher power. Basically our earthly life is a test. If we pass that test, we are promised eternal bliss. But there is a misconception about what constitutes that bliss. The hereafter is not like our earthly life. It is not sensual. The Quran says that women and men who do good will be given companionship that is pure, and will be surrounded by 70 virgins (beings of purity). Some people have misconstrued "purity" to mean virginity.

But years of experience as you grow and mature bring you to new levels of understanding. As a physician, sometimes I have wondered whether the Scriptures are real. But after extensive study, there's no question in my mind that the information in the Quran has come from a 'higher' source. Passage after passage in the Quran deals with space exploration, oceans and underwater life, fertilization followed by stages of embryo and fetus development, including explanations detailing when the embryo/fetus develops senses such as sight and hearing and so on. As a physician, I know that 1450 years ago, the technology didn't exist from which to draw that information.

The words of the Quran and all of its teachings, we believe to be the word of God transmitted directly from Him through the Angel Gabriel to prophet Mohammad (pbuh). As prophet Mohammed (pbuh) received these revelations, and because he was unable to read and write, he spoke them aloud and they were carefully transcribed by his companions. Over the 23 years that this took place, prophet Mohammed (pbuh) thought he was going mad. But even though he didn't understand what he was hearing, scholars in his community assured him that he was prophesying the word of God. So, for Muslims, the Quran is a great miracle and to this day, no one has been able to challenge its authenticity. All the instructions for life are in there.

In the Quran, God assures us that everyone makes mistakes, even the prophets. At some point, there comes a time when you examine your actions and think, "I wish I hadn't done that," or "I wish I had behaved differently." So ask for forgiveness. God is very merciful. At the same time, this doesn't justify making the same mistake over and over again, and asking for forgiveness for the same sins. For every action, there is a consequence.

The classic example in our faith is the story of Adam and Eve. We are taught that they were in heaven and they had free reign, both of them. And God said, "Do everything except don't go near the apple tree." They both disobeyed, and they both were punished. And the punishment was: leave heaven, go to Earth. And here we are, the descendents of Adam and Eve. They asked for forgiveness, they were forgiven, but there were consequences.

So understand that if you make a mistake, forgiveness doesn't necessarily mitigate the consequences. But the 114 chapters in the Quran start with: "In the name of God, the most gracious and most merciful." In the Islamic context, the concept of God and His mercy takes precedence over God and His punishment.

And remember: It is not for us to judge who is doing good, and who is not doing good. That is clearly outlined in the Quran. Don't pass judgment on others: to you, your way, to me, my way. Proselytizing is not permitted.

Islamic tradition says: live as if you're going to live forever. And live like you're going to die tomorrow. You've got to have both. Deen and dunya. Deen means faith. Dunya means world.

Live your faith and enjoy the world. In Islamic tradition, it is only with God's permission that we will die. You cannot predict the time for that. So be prepared. It can happen on the most unexpected day. In your 50s, you may be nowhere near your deathbed, but we are so often called to the mosque for those who have died unexpectedly.

As you move along, hopefully you mature. You learn more, you understand more. You become more introspective and less materialistic. You become more spiritual and do what you're expected to do in a more focused manner.

One way to do this is the Hajj. Once in a lifetime, a Muslim is expected to perform the pilgrimage of the Hajj, during the twelfth month of the lunar calendar. Muslims from every part of the world go to Mecca for this pilgrimage. It is usually for those who have made peace with their family issues, have some money to spare, and can take the trip to fulfill this requirement. You shouldn't have to take out a loan to do it. You do it when you have the assets, usually in your 40s or 50s.

Everyone wears the "ihram" which consists of two pieces of white sheets/towels. It's an amazing sight to see millions of people from all walks of life and diverse nationalities dressed in white. Everybody looks the same. And everyone is there for the same purpose: to ask for forgiveness; to ask for mercy from the Creator. It shakes you to the core.

Many people wish to perform the Hajj twice but only one is required. Perform another kind of good service to society. And at the end of each day, look in the mirror. Take a good look. What have you done all day, for yourself, for your family, for your neighbor, or your Creator? Try to do good. You may have made some mistakes, but you will have done some things well. Try to improve each day.

43

Trade strength for wisdom

Being the toughest person in the room is good. Being the most compassionate is better.

BY HAROLD S. KUSHNER

Kushner is Rabbi Laureate of Temple Israel, Natick, Mass., and the author of eight best-selling books, most notably When Bad Things Happen to Good People.

What is the wisdom we gain as we turn 50, wisdom that we may have lacked when we were younger? For men, we can stop seeing other men as rivals and come to see them as colleagues, perhaps even as students. At around age 50, we should begin to feel the need to mentor, to pass on what we have learned to a younger generation, lest all that experience vanish with us when our lives end. The fires of competitiveness have banked and we find it easier to relate to other men.

There is something profoundly gratifying, surprisingly so, about no longer seeing other men as rivals and obstacles to our success. Men in their 50s will find it easier to have male friends, not just buddies to fish with or watch a ballgame with, but real friends to share their innermost thoughts with, the way women have friends. An acquaintance of mine, a minister to a small church in a working-class suburb, confessed to me one day that when he turned 50, he realized to his embarrassment that he had spent the last 20 years hoping for one of his friends or colleagues to fall ill or be caught up in a scandal, so that he could apply to their more affluent church. Now he was prepared to give up that unworthy dream and become a mentor to younger ministers in the area. The thirst for success had given way to a concern for the lasting impact that he would have on the generation after him. I suspect it is not a coincidence that, when I was in my late 40s, I began to give fewer sermons and write books instead, and took on an assistant rabbi to whom I could be a mentor.

For a woman turning 50, the challenge is in a sense an opposite one, to move beyond living for and through others and focus more on oneself. If you have spent the first five decades of your life graduating from being someone's daughter to being someone's girlfriend to being someone's wife to being someone's mother and then grandmother, this can be a joyous time of discovery æ a time in your life to figure out what it would mean to be someone in your own right. You are not being selfish or irresponsible; you are reaching for wholeness.

The psychoanalyst Carl Jung suggested that every human infant has the potential for masculine and feminine dimensions to his or her personality. When society teaches little boys to be tough and ambitious and teaches little girls to be sensitive and live through others, it compels us to neglect half of our human potential. Mid-life, life after 50, is a time to go back and fill in the spaces we might have left blank when we were growing up.

My traditions teach me that wisdom is of greater value than physical strength, and that therefore we should rejoice when we reach that stage in our lives when physical agility begins to decline but wisdom increases.

The wisdom of middle age should include expanding your social network, making new friends to replace friends lost to distance or illness. It should include finding new interests, especially ones that stretch your mind. It should include a sense of obligation to give back to your community and your world some of what life has blessed you with. But most of all, it should include a sense of optimism, the feeling that, in the words of Robert Browning, "the best is yet to be, the last of life for which the first was made."

About the Editors

Allison Kyle Leopold, CONTRIBUTING EDITOR, is an award-winning editor and journalist, the owner and editor-in-chief of AKL Studio, a magazine and book development company, and editor of special interest publications for *Country Living Magazine.* She has authored more than a dozen books. Leopold began her career with *Seventeen Magazine* before joining *Harper's Bazaar* and *Vogue* magazines. She was editor of numerous special interest lifestyle publications for *Woman's Day,* travel editor of *Child* magazine, editor-in-chief of *Flair* magazine, and editor-in-chief of a regional magazine group.

Gerit Quealy, CONTRIBUTING EDITOR, is a journalist, author, and editor in New York City with extensive experience in the entertainment, travel, wellness, and lifestyle areas. The co-author of two books, *Fashion: Careers without College,* with Kathleen Beckett, and *Wedding Flowers* with Allison Kyle Leopold, Ms. Quealy is also the author of a humor book entitled *Are You My Husband?,* As deputy editor of AKL Studio Editorial, she has worked on projects for clients ranging from The Metropolitan Museum of Art to Avon, in addition to serving as senior editor at *Flair* magazine. She also writes regularly for *The New York Times.*

Debra Gordon, CONTRIBUTING EDITOR, is an award-winning journalist who has been writing about health and health-care for more than 15 years. She began her career as a reporter at the *Virginian Pilot* newspaper in Norfolk,

Virginia, then became the medical reporter at the *Orange County Register*, in Southern California. She has been a full-time freelance health and medical writer and editor since 2000, and has authored or co-authored numerous consumer health books. Her work has also appeared in *Health, Family Circle, Better Homes & Gardens, Good Housekeeping, Reader's Digest*, and *Diabetes Today* magazines.

Brian O'Connell, CONTRIBUTING EDITOR, is a Pennsylvania-based freelance writer and editor with 12 years experience covering political and business news and trends. A former Wall Street bond trader, he has contributed to dozens of national publications, including *The Chicago Tribune, The Wall Street Journal, Newsweek, Philadelphia Magazine, USA Weekend, Men's Health, Entrepreneur Magazine*, and *CBS News Market Watch*. He has authored 10 books, including two best-selling Book of the Month Club selections. In addition, O'Connell has appeared as an expert commentator on business and finance issues on CNN, International NewsFirst, Web TV, and Fox News.

Sarah Mahoney, SERIES EDITOR, is a contributing editor for *More, Parents*, and *Prevention*. Her work has appeared in *Woman's Day, Better Homes & Gardens, Reader's Digest*, and *The New York Times*. Now based in rural Maine, she formerly held several top-level editing positions at women's magazines, including editor of *Ladies' Home Journal*, editor-in-chief of *Fitness* magazine, and executive editor of *Parents* magazine. She started her career as a reporter at *Advertising Age* before joining United Press International as a business writer. She has made frequent television appearances, including Good Morning America, The Early Show, CNN, CBS, Court TV, Fox, Entertainment Tonight, and Lifetime.

Acknowledgements

For their help and support with this project, I would like
to thank Madeleine Beckman, Janet Cole, Vickie Peslak
Hyman, Michelle Keith, Dena Moss, Marie-Claire Sillick,
Jody Shields, and Robin Stern.

Allison Kyle Leopold

This book would not have been possible without the help
of the following people: Christopher Durang, Francis
Guinan, Jennifer Swihart, Gilda Squire, Charles Salzberg,
Giulia Melucci, Michael Gooch-Breault, Brian Shaffer,
Jensine Andresen, Melissa May, Steven May, Don Codling,
Mark K. Anderson, Sherry Anderson, Joanna Parson, Dee
Pelletier, Tom Kelly, Wendy Zoller, Rahadyan
Sastrowardoyo.

Gerit Quealy

I'd like to acknowledge the authors of the essays who will-
ingly submitted to several rounds of edits without complaining, and who volunteered so much of their time and
effort.

Debra Gordon

I'd like to thank the essayists who contributed their time and
efforts to this book. Each are at the top of their professions
and each brought a considerable amount of cachet to the
book. Special thanks also go to Elisabeth Flynn and
Gretchen Cassidy who proved invaluable in helping editing
and organizing the financial services and career management sections of the book.

Brian O'Connell